HERETIC SON

HERETIC SON

He Left Home and Church and Found
God in a U.S. Navy Destroyer

DONALD A. WEIR

authorHOUSE®

AuthorHouse™
1663 Liberty Drive
Bloomington, IN 47403
www.authorhouse.com
Phone: 1-800-839-8640

Published by AuthorHouse 5/17/2013

ISBN: 978-1-4817-5037-0 (sc)
ISBN: 978-1-4817-5036-3 (hc)
ISBN: 978-1-4817-5035-6 (e)

Library of Congress Control Number: 2013908233

Cover by Murder City Photography

This book is printed on acid-free paper.

DEDICATION
To Herbert and Esther Weir
Who always did the best they knew and
gave more than I will ever know.

And to Bev, Diane and Dave
For whom I learned too little and too late
how to be a husband and father.

"How sad it seems to me to leave this earth
without those you love the most
ever really knowing who you were."
Francesca in "The Bridges of Madison County.

ACKNOWLEDGMENTS

To the memory of Stanley Newcomb and Vivian Newport, who first saw the potential and nourished it. To John and John of University Associates, who cracked the shell and pushed the fledgling out of the nest. And, in no particular order a few of those whose books, tapes and lectures have guided me along The Way.

David N. Elkins, Ph.D.

Elizabeth Lesser

Karen Armstrong

Wayne Dyer

Grace Graziano

Mary Pipher

Lou Willett Stanek, Ph.D.

and

BARRY KIRSCH

Without whose weekly prodding at *The Summit* this book would never have found the page.

FOREWORD

In 2002 at the request of my family I wrote "They Called Me Padre", stories of a long life, many experiences and people. It related none of my inner life and lifelong pursuit of truth and meaning in a rapidly changing world. Perhaps there will be a sequel when I find the answers and the courage to set them to paper."

Thirteen years and many false starts and personal angst I offer "Heretic Son".

Maitland, Florida
May 2013

The past is not forgotten;
it isn't even past.
Our past shackles us, especially
when we don't realize it.
Understanding our past can re-open
roads that might have been taken,
but were not.

Harvey Cox
"The Future of Faith"

INTRODUCTION

"Tell me, Don, is your new book, "Heretic Son", fiction? Is it an autobiography? A memoir?"

"Yes it is!"

"Heretic Son" is a story. The story employs fact, fiction and fantasy to convey its message. Some of the names and places are authentic, some fantasy."

So, enjoy the story. You may meet someone you know. You may find yourself.

chapter one
COMING HOME

I crossed the Mississippi River at Dubuque. As the sun rose over my shoulder I felt the quiet power of the V-8 negotiating the hills of the old college town. I took a quick detour past the campus where I had spent seven years of my life. The old brick buildings evoked a flood of memories, of friends and faculty, classes and events. It was still the same place where I arrived sixty years ago, a stranger in a strange land. I departed with a pair of sheepskins that hardly passed for an education. I had no clear life goals, just an adaptive "go with the flow attitude" and a two year contract with the Navy. I did not tarry but headed back west on U.S. 20, the final leg of my journey from my home in Florida to Windom, Minnesota, and there attend the 60th anniversary of my high school graduation.

The road unrolled before me through endless miles of cornfields, farm buildings and all things Midwest. A sense of déjà vu rose in my belly and a long-forgotten adage surfaced in my memory: "You can take the boy off the farm, but you can't take the farm out of the boy".

At the intersection of Interstate 35, I turned north, set the cruise control on 70 and inserted a CD of Yo Yo Ma's cello classics. Yo Yo made a great traveling companion, allowing my mind to process the implications of this trip. Would I be shunned by the community for straying from the ways of my parents? Would the speaker preach the "prodigal son"? Would I be shut out of my classmates' informal gatherings? As I crossed the state line into Minnesota I swapped YO YO for Glenn Miller, and turned west again on I-90 for another uninterrupted 90 minutes of cornfields, cattle farms, concrete and concert. Roadside signs named nearby towns and villages unremembered these many years: Albert Lea, Blue Earth, Fairmont, Welcome, Alpha and Sherburn, each evoking a dormant memory of times gone by. Glenn Miller was playing all the 40's standards; "Tuxedo Junction", "In the Mood", "Blue Moon" and "Moonlight Serenade", tunes we danced to at the proms and the jukeboxes. These were the songs of my teens, songs popular when I walked and worked these lands.

As I drove on my mind turned to the letter in the attaché case at my side. I had memorized the brief contents of the two terse paragraphs:

Windom High School
Windom, Minnesota 56101
March 2, 2006

Mr. Donald A. Weir
1955 Weeping Willow Way
Orlando, Florida 32817

Dear Mr. Weir,

Earlier this year our senior social studies class read and discussed your bestselling book, "Life 101". The book has initiated both a lively classroom discussion and a petition to the administration to invite you to be their commencement speaker on June 6, 2006. The faculty and administration have concurred with their choice, and in addition, we have voted to bestow upon you Windom High School's "Alumnus of Distinction" award given on rare occasions to a WHS graduate who has earned national recognition for his or her life's work. We note that this will also be the sixtieth anniversary of your graduating class, an appropriate occasion to celebrate so we sincerely hope you will be able to accept our invitation.

While we are unable to provide an honorarium for your service, we will reimburse your travel expenses and make reservations for your stay in Windom. We look forward to your early response.

Sincerely,

s/ Rodger F. Hill, Superintendent

I smiled and thought, it's not the Pulitzer Prize or the Silver Star but it is still nice to be recognized in the hometown.

I had accepted the invitation impulsively with little thought of what I would be saying to the seventy-or-so seventeen and eighteen-year olds who would be impatiently waiting to grab their diplomas and flee the world of WHS forever. Sixty years had not dimmed my memory of my graduation night. I had squirmed in my chair, my mind set on the double date that Bob and I had arranged to take a couple of cheerleaders to Arnold's Park amusement center, a proper celebration of our graduation.

Now, six decades later and watching the well-remembered and endless acres of farm land bisected by this strip of concrete I thought, what do I have in common with these young people and their families? Why had the Board invited the "Rebel of the class of '46", the "Heretic Son of the Church"? What can I say that will assist these teens in their transition from adolescents to adults, help them find their individual paths to a meaningful life? Years of public speaking experience had given me confidence that I could cobble up a few inspiring thoughts , perhaps give some word that will point at least one or two young people to a path of success and fulfillments; something more than the typical "Rah-rah, go get 'em for God and country." Will they, like I was, be anxiously waiting their turn to grab the diploma and run out to celebrate?" What few words do I have to say to the class of '06 that may help them into the next chapter of their lives, something that they will remember after the day's ceremonies?"

The mental tapes of the past began replaying random scenes from years of college and seminary, the ordination and years of ministry, of sermons and baptisms and funerals and weddings, the wrenching departure from the Church and the transition into the world of business, the rapid rise from sales to management to development of a successful and profitable enterprise. It had been a long, circuitous road from Windom and its people, a road often marked by stress and trauma for me and my family. My innards began to churn. Would encounter those strident voices, with mixed emotions? Would I encounter those same strident, judgmental voices?

I had had little contact with the home town since the death of my parents. Most of my relatives and my classmates were now dead, incapacitated or relocated. I gave silent thanks for good longevity genes and a healthy lifestyle that have kept me in reasonable health at the age of seventy seven.

As I reached the off-ramp for U.S. 71 North, the clock on the dashboard read 2:21 p.m. and I switched off the cruise control, lowered the windows, muted Glenn Miller and inhaled deeply the essence of springtime in Minnesota. The fragrance of the first cut of alfalfa blended with the pungent scent of fertile farm soil enriched by the droppings of two hundred Black Angus cattle.

To my left a solitary farmer was cultivating eight rows of hybrid corn, riding in the air-conditioned cab of the familiar green and yellow John Deere tractor. Gone were the quarter-section farmsteads staked out by immigrants under a tree claim one hundred years ago. Gone were the farm buildings protected from winter blizzards by a grove of cottonwoods and elm. In their place were fields of six or seven hundred acres, without tree, without fence or building.

A rise in the road afforded an unobstructed view of a typical livestock farm with its signature white-trimmed red barn and twin silos, a pleasant contrast to the fields of grain. About a hundred head of Blank Angus steaks-to-be were feeding lazily at racks laden with alfalfa.

Over the years I had told myself that I no longer have roots here, but the farm boy of the 1930s and 40s welled up inside me and an inner voice cried out "Home!"

A few miles farther a sign on a small bridge declared, "Des Moines River"; soon followed by another, "Windom City Limits, population 4197, County Seat of Cottonwood County". A Native Son has returned.

As I slowed into town, some of the landmarks were vaguely familiar although new businesses and houses had extended the town's perimeter. Bearing right onto Lakeside Street, and then turning right again, I crossed under the aluminum arch bearing the words: LAKESIDE CEMETERY. Here sleep my ancestors and the town fathers and mothers of several generations. Here lie the pioneers who transformed the raw prairies into productive farms and picturesque villages. Everywhere there are vases off fresh cut flowers amid lilacs and other blooming landscape, evidence of the recent Memorial Day observance.

I allowed the Caddy to idle down the grassy lane that separated rows of gray and brown granite markers bearing once-familiar names:

KEITH
Douglas and Hazel

Doug was editor of the weekly "Cottonwood County Citizen" and an elder in the Presbyterian Church, Hazel was the church musician.

NELSON
Oscar and Inez.

Oscar was the president of the bank and Inez a church

musician also. They were parents of my very close friend in high school.

KELLER

Albert and Myrtle.

Albert, owner of a trucking business; Myrtle was renowned for her cooking at church suppers. Close friends of my parents. And beside them lay,

KELLER

Russell

Their eldest son and high school basketball star, lost in a troop ship bound for Europe and torpedoed by a German U-Boat in the icy waters of the North Atlantic.

NELSON

Clarence and Celia

Owner of gas station and retail delivery of fuel to farmers; tractors and engines.
and next to them:

NELSON

William, 1ˢᵗ Lieutenant U.S.ARMY

Their only son and West Point graduate, felled on some frozen and unremembered Korean hill.
I turned right again coming to the substantial grey granite stone:

KANE

Joseph and Anna

My maternal grandparents.

Continuing down a gentle slope to my destination; I cut the engine at these brown granite headstones:

WEIR
Henry and Emma

My paternal grandparents and next to them

WEIR
Herbert and Esther

My parents.

All four were staunch Presbyterians. All born, lived and died scratching out a living from the stubborn Midwestern soil during the Great Depression. These were true pioneers, people of the land enduring drought, hail storms, blizzards, and disease! They built schools and churches, living the American dream, and rearing families by long established customs and rituals.

The silence of the moment was broken only by a gentle breeze whispering through the lilacs and blue spruce. A pair of robins lunched among the stone markers. Unbidden tears filled my eyes, for I had come here with intent. I planted my feet on native soil, opened my laptop and began to write:

"Owning our story and loving ourselves through that process is the bravest thing that we will ever do."
Brene Brown

chapter two
CRIME AND PUNISHMENT

Dear Mom and Dad,

I suppose that I have written those words a thousand times, from high school summer camp, from seven years of college and seminary, from fifty years of travels around the world, in ships and stations and continents. My thoughts have always turned towards home, to you. I have shared many of these thoughts, but I have held back the ways in which I was growing away from some of your beliefs, some of the teachings of the church and my inner struggle to find truths and creeds that I could believe and live.

There was within me a hidden voice, an inner voice trying to be heard. There were always these unspoken thoughts, the subjects that I felt were taboo in your life, the hidden issues and unvoiced complaints that have remained unexpressed and unresolved unto this day. And I guess (I?) wanted to avoid your disapproval and disappointment. I waited for some word of approval, some sanction of a life and lifestyle so foreign to you and kept hidden from you. So I came here today to speak openly about those unspoken thoughts and feelings, and perhaps find the peace that has eluded me.

First, I often felt that I was unjustly punished.

Mom, do you remember...................?

September 1934.

It has been over seventy years, but this memory still stings. At 4:15 p.m. the rickety homemade school bus, constructed of wood siding bolted to the frame of an ancient Chevy truck, ground to a stop at our rural mailbox. I lunged forward, vaulting through the door, hurdled the three steps down and landed in the rich native soil of our Midwestern farmland. Home! A narrow lane of two rutted tracks stretched from the mail box some quarter of a mile towards the house surrounded by a cluster of other farm buildings and set in the midst of 320 acres of cornfields, oats, flax and pasture. I started down that lane passing the freshly plowed grain field on the left, the third crop of lush alfalfa on the right, a giant cottonwood tree and a small apple orchard midway. It was one of those magnificent autumn days, a cloudless azure sky and the fragrance of fertile loam blending with the smell of lilacs and decaying apples. It was a "Huck Finn" kind of day, too nice a day to spend in school, and much too nice to face the farm chores awaiting me. I paused at the orchard, set the metal lunch box on the ground, retrieved the remains of a half-eaten apple and shinned up an apple tree. There I reclined comfortably in the crotch formed by the lower limbs, bit into the apple, and let the juice flow down my chin. Two blackbirds chatted nosily on the next tree, waiting to feast on the apple's core. The late afternoon sun warmed my back. My mind wandered back to the story of Tom Sawyer that our teacher had been reading to us, imagining how great it would be to play hooky from school with a friend like Huck Finn, to ignore the calls of Aunt Polly and just watch the tugs and barges make their way slowly upstream with cargo from distant places.

My reverie was abruptly interrupted by my mother's high pitched voice: "Donald Allan Weir, get down from that tree and get up here this minute!" End of dream! Back to reality! She had seen the bus in the distance and rightfully expected me in the house within the next ten minutes. I scrambled down the tree, grabbed my lunch box and the take-home art project upon which one of the blackbirds had accurately deposited a messy blob tinted by the plums he had stolen from the neighbor's orchard.

"Where have you been? What have you been doing? It has been twenty minutes since that bus went by and you know you are supposed to come straight home and get your chores done."

Without a pause for my answer she continued, "Who do you think you are, mister, someone special? I think you are getting too big for your britches, and it's time to bring you down a peg or two". And with one swift, sure, practiced move she bent me over her leg and delivered several well-placed swats with her work-hardened hand. "Now get your clothes changed and get out to the barn and hop to your chores."

I ran to the house, ran up the stairs, and changed from my school pants into the striped bib overalls, standard uniform of farm males age 3-70. The chores! Always the goddamned chores! Before school, after school, morning and night seven days a week, the damned chores! No complaining, no sass, and no backtalk, just get at it: clean the barn, scoop out cow manure, feed the animals, milk the cows, feed the hogs and sheep and chickens. The damned chores! And all the while my friends who lived in town were playing ball, hanging out at the general store, listening to "The Lone Ranger" and "Jack Armstrong" on the radio. Damn the chores!

Too big for my britches? You damned right I am. Somebody special? You damned right I am. I am one of a kind, born with a unique set of talents, commissioned to make a difference in the world. But keep that to myself "if I know what's good for me.

APRIL 1938: Leroy was my first real friend, a classmate in sixth grade. We would sneak cigarettes from his dad and smoke in the school's boiler room, talk about girls, exchange bad information about sex and spin fantasies about our futures. So it was a rare day, a day to remember when I was allowed to invite Leroy to ride the bus home and spend the night with me on the farm. I was unexpectedly given a pass on my chores so Leroy and I headed out through the pasture to one of my favorite places, the slough. We watched muskrats building their two-story houses in the water. We tried to snare a gopher and just enjoyed being boys of ten.

The state was building a new highway that abutted the south

boundary of our farm and they had installed a 48-inch culvert under the road bed. That seemed to us like an interesting place to explore so we stooped down and proceeded, finding frogs, crickets, worms and of course, mud.

When it began to grow dark we headed back toward the house, now a mile or so away, chatting away, throwing stones and enjoying a sense of carefree freedom that Tom Sawyer would have envied. It was nearly dark when we finally reached the house where we were met with the wrath of both my parents who thought we should have been home long ago. "Where have you been?" they screamed. "We have been out driving around looking for you, honking the horn and calling your names"! They had imagined the worst, that we had drowned in the slough or been kidnapped or any other dire fates that they could have imagined. Dad took me to the basement and gave me a man-sized spanking while my friend stood by and protested as he watched.

"We didn't do anything bad, we just walked around looking at things", he said, and which did not register at all with Dad. I was humiliated and thought that I had done nothing wrong, and was given no chance to explain. It was becoming obvious that my opinion was not worth hearing. Seventy-five years later Madeline Levine would write in the New York Times, "A loving parent is warm, willing to set limits and unwilling to breach a child's psychological boundaries by invoking shame or guilt. Parents must acknowledge their own anxiety". Alas, too late for my shame.

Many years later this scene flashed across my mind when I heard a comedian quip: "Until I was 14 years old I thought my first name was 'Shut Up'".

Mom and Dad, when I became the parent of small children, I began to appreciate your anxiety and response, but I still think the punishment and embarrassment were much too severe for a ten-year old boy in front of his best friend.

This scenario was not unique to my parents. They were doing what their parents had done. In fact, it seemed that the whole community mindset was that of adults conspiring to police and to enforce the accepted mores of the community. "Spare the rod and spoil the child" the oft-quoted Biblical mandate was embraced and practiced with vigor. Common currency dictated, "Give a child a few good thrashings to create character and respect for adults." Corporal punishment was accepted in schools and teachers spanked students with impunity. Every child and parent knew the words to the song, "School Days".

"School days, school days,
Good old golden rule days,
Reading and writing and 'rithmatic,
taught to the tune of the hickory stick…."

Dad, do you remember the lost spade incident?

On the farm we had the usual array of tools that each of us used as necessary to perform the many activities of farming. One day Dad needed to use the spade, an elongated shovel used mostly to make draining ditches. Unable to find the spade he remembered seeing me use it recently and assumed that I had lost it. Unable prove my innocence I was automatically guilty and got another licking and verbal abuse about taking care of things. Months later I overheard him telling someone that he had found the spade where he had left it, but never let me know or, God forbid, apologize for the unwarranted licking.

Then there was the time I shot the muskrats. My brother Jim and I had received a Winchester, single shot, .22 rifle for Christmas. When we had been well instructed in its use we were allowed, one at a time, to take the gun with 5 or 6 bullets out for target practice or to shoot predatory birds and rodents around the farm. One fine day I took the rifle out in the pasture, presumably to shoot gophers whose burrows ravaged the pasture. My wanderings took me to the slough where muskrats were busily building their fascinating homes in the water. To me, they were just another pest so I shot and killed three of them, then, launching a little scow, retrieved their bodies to examine then leave lying in the pasture fence row. I had been secretly observed by a neighbor who dutifully reported the incident to Dad who called me into the house and questioned, accused, and lectured me that I had broken the law, slain a valuable and innocent creature. I remember looking at his belt buckle at my eye level as he ranted a long and convoluted sentence with double negatives, split infinitives and dangling participles that ended with a question that demanded a yes-or-no answer, and threatened to turn me over to the sheriff as he would other lawbreakers. I knew right from wrong but was lost in his syntax, not understanding the question so I took a 50-50 chance and answered "yes". That triggered another verbal explosion and I muttered "no, no". I don't remember the punishment, only that I did not go to jail or receive the ever-present razor strap across my backside. I was probably denied access to the rifle for a time with the warning, "If you know what's good for you, you will not let this happen again!" What's good for me indeed! I doubt if it is humiliation, belittling or spanking. I had been encouraged to kill squirrels, crows, rabbits and gophers, not a big difference to a ten-year old. It was also about that time that I heard my grandmother ranting about my cousin's behavior. "He needs a good shaking!" she declared. One more evidence of the code!

These scenes were not unique to my parents. They did what had been done to them. These were the standards and mores of the times and of the community. "Children should be seen and not heard" was a frequently quoted proverb and believed by most. And in a broader sense, these are the standards of the rest of world: the strongest, the loudest, the richest voices, be they individuals, institutions or nations, the strongest, loudest, and richest make and enforce the laws for the rest of the world, locally and internationally. It was the standard of many homes, of schools, on the playground, in churches, and reinforced in my gentle mind on a regular basis. In my mind I heard again and again, "Who do you think you are, Mister? Just shut up and do as you are told! "And, I believe that this is the ethic that gave birth to the gun culture we have inherited, and the philosophy of international relations and the cause of wars. In this culture I learned the practice of avoidance and retreat to an inner and silent life of shelter.

This bullying found reinforcement and justification in the academic world such as Dr. John Watson's 1928 book, "Psychological Care of Infant and Child". He advocated strict schedules and carefully doled-out affection. "Never, never kiss your child" he warned. "Never hold it in your lap. Never rock its carriage."

Years later the power of these practices would show up as my reluctance to speak out in groups, even when I knew that I had a better solution, a better idea. That inner voice still echoed, "Who do you think you are, Mister. Shut up and do as you're told!" It would be years before the appearance of Dr. Benjamin Spock's revolutionary book, "The Common Sense book of Baby and Child Care" which encouraged parents to trust their common sense, their instincts, and their unique knowledge and feelings for their own babies. "Don't take too seriously all that the neighbors say. Don't be overawed by what the experts say. Don't be afraid to trust your own common sense," Spock wrote. Alas, too late for depression born babies.

chapter three
PUBLICALLY HUMILIATED

Dad and Mom, I sometimes felt that I was singled out for embarrassment, to entertain the big people and that no one cared about my feelings.

One Sunday when I was a tyke of 4 or 5, our family was at my maternal grandparent's home for a family gathering. My mother was one of seven siblings so the place was swarming with aunts, uncles and cousins. Grandma walked with the aid of a cane so she sat where she could greet and see everyone. As I ran past her she used the hook end of her cane to snag my ankle, trip me, then held me down, and for the amusement of all present, she tickled me until I cried. No one came to my aid, no one protested, everyone laughed.

Later that day, cigar-smoking loud mouth Uncle Alex who had once seen a buck sheep chase me across the farmyard, retold and embellished that story, stating that "if I had run another half mile I would have killed the sheep with exhaustion", and then led the group in laughter. The same loud mouth uncle shouted across

the room, "What time did you get up this morning, Donnie?"
As a 4 year old I answered, "Hast past four", at which he roared
and he then repeated it in the parlor for the entertainment of all,
guffawing loudly at his own humor.

Another incident in which I felt publically shamed occurred
in the first grade of school. There were just four of us boys
in the class, and at recess time we played together. One day
Clyde brought a tin of Copenhagen snuff from home and we four
sneaked into the abandoned shell of a school bus in a far corner
of the school grounds where the contraband snuff was generously
shared and imbibed. Later in the day my three classmates became
violently sick, vomiting up the evidence of our youthful sins. They
were sent home with notes to parents detailing the transgressions
of their sons. For some unknown reason I was spared the illness,
so remained in school and to my gratitude both my brother Jim
and sister Emmy kept silent at home about the incident.

Some months later on a Saturday evening later I was with
Mother shopping in a general store .Thee we encountered my
teacher and she greeted me with, "How is my little chewer this
evening?" Naturally Mom asked the meaning of that remark,
so the whole story was loudly and publically recited to my total
embarrassment and shame, and to the amusement of numerous
shoppers who like vultures had moved in to feast on this morsel
of gossip. I wanted to drop through the floor. I think I wet my
pants. And of course when we arrived home the whole incident
was related to Dad. It was late and I was sent to bed with the
promise that this would be dealt with later.......giving me more
time to worry and repent. My parents must have found some
hidden humor in that episode as I was awarded only minor
detention.

I was about eight or nine years of age when Dad began calling
me "Goofus". He may have meant it as a term of affection, but
I thought it meant goofy, slow witted, dippy or stupid. In true
conflict-avoidance mode I buried my feelings and kept my mouth
shut about it. Then one hot summer afternoon I was doing my

damned chores, carrying two buckets of water from the well to the chicken house, he called to me at some distance across the farm yard, "Goofus!" I ignored his call and kept on walking. Then he shouted loudly, GOOFUS! I stopped in my tracks, turned and yelled back at the top of my lungs, "MY NAME IS NOT GOOFUS!", and kept on walking. That was the last time I ever heard that moniker and memorably the only time I "talked back" and got away with it. Of course, there was never an apology or acknowledgment of the resentment and humiliation he had caused me for weeks, the emotional damage that still seems fresh in my memory. Why was I not called by the name he had given me? Why were not my siblings also given demeaning nicknames? Why do I recall it with such clarity today?

It was late afternoon years later at age 36, I was on duty at McMurdo Station, Antarctica. Most of the officers were gathered for Happy Hour in the Quonset hut that served as officers' quarters. The captain, a grizzly and profane old sea dog well into his second bourbon began to tease and taunt me in front of the whole group. He had been at chapel service where I delivered a very low key plea for making this year of isolated duty an opportunity for spiritual growth. "You'll never catch 'em with that soft sell, Padre. Your predecessor was out on the ice shelf driving a D-9 bulldozer, not sitting in the office, reading his Bible."

I took a deep breath and responded, "I grew up on a farm and can still operate every piece of equipment manufactured by John Deere, but I acquired nineteen years of formal education and the church did not ordain me or the Navy commission me to plow snow. When the mail comes and Joe Seabee gets a 'Dear John' or the death of the cook's mother arrives by telegram, neither you nor they will have to hunt me down on the ice shelf . As far as the sermon goes, if you are looking for a Billy Graham, you've got the wrong boy. I tend to follow the one who taught, "Blessed are the poor in spirit, blessed are the meek, blessed are the peacemakers...."

The Old Man began again, but there is no arguing with a drunk, especially when he is your boss. I excused myself and left for dinner. My blood pressure was up. I felt toyed with to the entertainment of the other officers. In the middle of that night I experienced a gut-wrenching nightmare in which I was fighting with Dad, down on the floor beating on him. I awoke in a sweat, shaking uncontrollably, shamed that I should even think of such a deed, even if he had called me Goofus.

"A survey of psychologists states it is important to forgive parents and others for your mental health."
Lewis M. Andrews, Ph.D.

chapter four
MIDDLE CHILD

I often felt like a second class member of the family, caught between Jim the Crown Prince, Heir to the Throne, and Emmy, the long-awaited Princess in Pink.

Jim was born exactly three years and twenty-four days before me, the first child, the first son and the first paternal grandson and guarantor that the family name would be continued. He was adored by all and was the center of everyone's attention. Three years later my birth was greeted with, "Oh, another boy! He will make a good farm hand. And we already have plenty of Jim's outgrown clothes for him."

Then, at the ripe old age of nine months and notably before I was properly weaned, we were pregnant with the "Princess". I was summarily removed from the maternal breast and attention was focused on "The Coming Event". Of course there was great celebration at the birth of Emmy Lou. No hand-me-down-clothes for Her! She had usurped both my role as "the baby" and my place at the primeval source of nourishment and cuddling, leaving me to live in the shadow of my brother's accomplishments and Her Highness. I was frequently referred to as Weir's other boy or Jim's little brother. Everything I did, Jim had already done, and no doubt, better. And everything that she did was cute and sweet. Years later I would read in Dr. Kevin Leman's "The Birth Order Book", comments about the position of middle children: "They were born too late to get the privileges and special treatment the first born seemed to inherit by right. And they were born too soon to strike the bonanza that many last-borns enjoy, the relaxing of the disciplinary reins which are sometime translated into 'getting away with murder."

Long before psychologists figured out the significance of birth order or coined the term "middle child syndrome", I was destined to live out a classic example of that yet-to-be formulated theory. In my effort to find recognition I would become the rebel, not with outrageous behavior, but simply ignoring custom, tradition and expectations, and living by my own vision. I would be the first out of the nest, the first to attend college, the child to adopt a lifestyle alien to both family and the local community, and ultimately the one to kick over the traces of the church and its rigid dogmas. Frank J. Sulloway writes of the middle child in his book, "Born to Rebel:" "Later- borns are more inclined than firstborns to question authority and to resist pressure to conform to a consensus.....more risk orientated....more likely to engage in dangerous physical activities or 'clown-around', playing the buffoon."

Child psychologists concur that "The middle child is often a loner, uncomfortable in groups and marked with a sense of not belonging or out of place". I don't consider myself a typical loner, but I have at least learned to become as comfortable in solitude as I am in groups, especially loud, confrontational and argumentative groups.

The Sunday routine on the farm during my early years serves to illustrate the fact. Sundays began like the other six days of the week, early rising, milking cows, feeding and cleaning up after the animals before breakfast. Next, get washed and dressed for Sunday School and Church services then home to a bounteous dinner. Only after dinner, could we begin to observe "the day of rest", a few brief hours before chores. If it was a typical Minnesota spring day I would head out to explore the pasture and the slough (a pond that was home to muskrats, bullheads, and frogs, and the watering hole for numerous species of birds and rodents. I was alone but always accompanied by Shep, a mixed breed shepherd, my constant companion and confidant. When we had moved out of view of the farm buildings, away from the eyes and ears of parents we would lie in the grass, watch fluffy cumulous clouds drift overhead; listen to the song of a meadowlark perched on the barbed wire fence, and watch a family of muskrats building its intricate home in the water. A red winged blackbird sat atop a cattail swaying in the breeze. I basked in the warmth of the sun. The hillside adorned with a blanket of Mayflowers and my senses overflowed with the sights, sounds and smells of creation. No chores here! No "SHUT UP!" No humiliating relatives! No" Goofus"! Shep lay beside me, ears pricked up to catch every sound, his nostrils twitching with a hundred scents of nature beyond my ability to detect. The words of the Psalmist, memorized during years of Sunday School and Vacation Bible School floated into my consciousness: "The earth is the Lord's and the fullness thereof…..Consider the lilies of the field, they neither sew nor spin, yet your heavenly father cares for them"…."When I consider the heavens, the moon and stars which Thou hast ordained, what is man….."

Many years later I would recall such an afternoon when I discovered the opening lines of

I also wondered if Robert Frost was a middle child, writing… "The Pasture"

> *I'm going out to clean the pasture spring;*
> *I'll only stop to rake the eaves away*
> *(And wait to watch the water clear, I may:*
> *I shan't be long.---You come too."*

Winter Sundays provided their own special times of solitude. If there was either a blizzard or a rain storm, I would ascend to my bedroom after dinner and read farm magazines, outdoor sporting magazines, or back issues of National Geographic, Reader's Digest or Good Housekeeping, all handed off by generous relatives and friends of greater means. In "Fur, Fish and Game" I learned to trap mink and muskrats, and smoke badgers from their dens and skunks from their holes, all solitary activities. "National Geographic" magazine instilled a lifetime of exploring the beauties and wonders of our country plus much of Europe, Asia, and remote regions of the world. I studied the globe, maps and photos of these places, only dreaming that I would someday set foot on four of the seven continents. The extensive reading also provided a sense of how to string words together conveying pictures, ideas and narrative, a talent that has served me well for a lifetime.

These solitary hours honed both my reading skills and curiosity about a broad range of subjects. Years later I would identify with Shelby Foote who wrote of his childhood: "My father died just before I turned six years old, so I've been a latchkey kid before there were any latchkey kids, and I liked it. Cast on my own resources I began to read very early and with great pleasure.....Getting close to books, and spending time by myself, I was obliged to think about things I would never have thought about if I was busy romping around with a brother and sister."

Other symptoms of the middle child syndrome were playing out as well. Both of my siblings inherited their mother's musical talent. Mother had played both the piano and the violin, had a lovely voice and sang in the church choir. Jim, with no training in music, purchased an accordion, taught himself to play. By age fourteen he could play by ear any tune he had heard. He also played trombone in the high school band and later in life would direct choirs, sing in barbershop quartets and sing at many funerals. Emmy took piano lessons, played clarinet in the high school band, sang in the high school chorus and in later life purchased an electronic organ for her home. On the other hand, I inherited Dad's tin ear. Neither of us could carry a tune and after trying several instruments I gave up the futile effort to make music. I sang (quietly) in the church choir which satisfied my social needs but contributed nothing to the liturgy. I felt like Arthur Miller who wrote of his middle child experience in "Timebends": "I was caught between Joan, who had clearly taken my place as chief baby, and my brother, whose stature I could not begin to match."

Dr. Leman wrote further in his "Birth Order Book", "As I have counseled middle-born children, they have often told me they did not feel that special growing up. The first born had his place and the baby of the family had his special spot, but the middle child may have been the overlooked child, the taken for granted child. There just didn't seem to be that much room or even a great deal of parental awareness of the need for a spot on the pecking order." It was this drama that would lead me to break away from home and community, acquire an education and a life far from the one into which I had been born. Over the seven decades, I have grown much more comfortable in my own skin, in my own identity and more understanding, tolerant of my parents, realizing that they were doing the best they could, the best they knew how. But the lingering memories of the middle child role do not die easily.

I was born into the age of the Great Depression. Dad and his dad had lost their farm by foreclosure when the value of the farm dropped below the amount of the mortgage: "under water" in today's lingo. We then moved to a rental farm, essentially a share- crop where the landlord, an insurance company that had foreclosed on this land, received 40% of the proceeds from the grain sold, and the tenant, our parents, received 60%, some of which was sold, most of it fed to the cattle, hogs and chickens. The farm always provided us with plenty to eat: milk, eggs, beef, chicken and vegetables from a generous garden, but spending money was hard to come by. The essentials such as sugar, flour and spices for the kitchen plus gasoline, oil and repairs for machinery, seed corn and veterinary bills were priorities. New clothing for the second son was mostly out of the question, especially with slightly worn clothing outgrown by the firstborn. But during the years I was ages 6 to 12, I knew nothing about and cared nothing for the depression, the financial struggles of my parents to keep the family fed, clothed and warm during the Minnesota winters. I only knew that I got the hand-me-downs and they got new clothes. They received the attention. I often felt ignored, except, of course, at chore time.

*To be nobody but yourself in a world which is doing its best,
night and day, to make you everybody else,
means to fight the hardest battle to which any
human being can fight; and never stop fighting."*
e.e. cummings

chapter five
GIRLS

You often shamed me and criticized me for showing any interest in girls. I became shy, awkward and inept as I later tried to relate to the opposite sex.

The classroom desks in Wilder school were of typical design of the time; the front of my desk formed the back of the person next in front of me. In fifth grade I found myself looking at dark brown hair cut in bangs and a scattering of freckles on the nape of her neck. She was cute in a plump, Scandinavian sort of way. I showed my interest in typical fifth-grade boy fashion, touching, poking, tickling and passing notes of affection. She blushed, feigned disgust and displeasure, but betrayed her true feeling with smiles and keeping near me at recess. Likewise I found ways to be near her in games, on adjoining swings and pursuing and catching her while playing tag.

Our mutual interest was duly noted by the other kids and they were soon chanting, "Donnie's got a girlfriend! Donnie's got a girlfriend!" One evening at home my sister took up that chant, "Donnie's got a girlfriend!" That triggered my parents' grand inquisition. "Who is this girl? What are you doing with her? What did you say to her? Why do you think we are sending you to school? You're too young to be thinking about girls, so just settle down and study in school or you will wish you had. I don't want to hear anything more about you playing with this girl or teasing her!" Yes Ma'am!

Of course this did not inhibit nature's normal instincts. It just drove them underground. Now I had to sneak opportunities to pursue my interests, carefully avoid the eyes of siblings, peers and parents. In seventh grade, probably age twelve or thirteen, I developed a "crush" on one of Emmy's friends and fifth grade classmate. It was a textbook case of puppy love. I lived on the farm, she lived in town so there was no opportunity to carry her books home or see her on weekends. She was in fifth grade and I was in seventh so there was little opportunity to see more than an occasional glance of her at school. She attended the Baptist Church and I attended the Presbyterian. Our "romance", our "relationship" consisted of passing notes through my sister (now an ally), some smiles and winks as we caught glimpses of each other in the halls or across the room in assembly.

In our community like most rural villages, every Saturday night farmers came to town to trade their fresh produce, eggs and meat for canned goods and such staples as flour and sugar. It was also a time to visit with neighbors, exchange information about crops, livestock, recipes and gossip. Teens and older children were allowed to assemble at ice cream and soda shops, attend movies and use the playgrounds. The young lady and I agreed to a rendezvous at a designated spot and then take a walk through a residential area, away from the shopping and entertainment areas and away from the eyes of parents and their adult allies. We probably spent only fifteen or twenty minutes together, and all I remember of that "date" was that she talked non-stop. Our "relationship" came to an abrupt end when she mailed a valentine to me and had written on it, "I Love You". Mother intercepted the card that was plainly addressed to me, opened it and then confronted me with the evidence, as if I had committed the mortal sin of the century. She shamed and lectured me to have nothing more to do with this girl and to "be a good boy". "You are too young to be carrying on like this". Everything but Hester Prynne's Scarlet Letter!

Again I drew deeper into my shell, played the good boy role, but teen testosterone would not be denied, only driven into clandestine expressions. Now I must be more careful, more secretive about future contacts with the opposite sex. Nonetheless, the continual teasing, lecturing, forbidding and threatening imprinted my tender psyche with shyness and shame. Parents' rules and rulings were reinforced including our church's prohibition of dancing which excluded me from proms, sock-hops and homecoming dances.

It is difficult now to imagine the morals and mores of those days except as still practiced by a handful of sects in rural areas. I never saw my dad show affection to my mother, no hugs, never a kiss. I had no model of affection between men and women, boys and girls, only prohibitions, threats and dire warnings. Discussions of divorce, puberty, or dating were taboo. I once overheard women relatives whispering in the kitchen about my cousin who was getting a divorce. It was considered a sin and a shame for the family never to be mentioned in the presence of my juvenile ears. But that was life on a rural farm in 1940. Who could have imagined a day of "R" rated movies shown in the living room, condoms, tampons and EPT kits displayed at the checkout counter.

I was totally unprepared for my first nocturnal emission, "a wet dream". It was weeks before I understood the meaning of the starch that appeared in the crotch of my pajamas. Later, in the school locker room I heard the explanation in teenage vernacular. Another mystery was revealed when I stumbled upon a pamphlet that a teacher had handed to my sister explaining menstruation.

The basic facts of reproduction were visible everywhere on the farm. I had witnessed the reproductive acts of cattle, horses, pigs, sheep and chickens. I had midwifed the birth of all of them, but there was no model of human courting or lovemaking between man and woman, only whispered gossip and Western movies. It was only from older students in the school locker rooms that these matters were discussed in crude, vulgar terms and apocryphal accounts of female anatomy and sexual conquest. At home there was talk of the weather, of the farm work, of the neighbors, but no talk of being a family, no hugs, no encouragement. I'm sure our parents were preoccupied with staying alive, with feeding, clothing and housing the five of us, many of their own dreams crushed by the Great Depression, the loss of their land and with it much of their self-esteem. They were unschooled in coping with adolescent behavior.

Later, at college, away from parental prohibitions, I had grown so shy and socially inept that I failed to take advantage of the opportunities presented by several hundred lovely girls on campus. My classmates who had learned to dance and date in high school happily seized the opportunities for cheap coke dates, free concerts, recitals and ball games on campus. My skills included milking a cow, harnessing and driving a team of horses, midwifing a litter of pigs and operating farm machinery and equipment. Through four years of college and three years of graduate school I had only a few casual, awkward dates. I would face another ten years of self-doubt, inferior self-image and unsatisfying encounters with the fairer sex. It was not until my thirtieth year and I was a respected naval officer and clergyman but still socially "hung up" that a shipmate introduced me to my future wife. He arranged a blind date to a wardroom dinner party with the lovely daughter of his neighbor. With no one to pass judgment or criticize we continued to court. She was accepting of my awkward ways, her family also accepted me as I was, welcomed me into their home. As we courted I made clear to her and her family the inconveniences, and sometimes hardships, of the itinerant life of a Navy man, but their affections were undeterred. We married and have lived "happily ever after". She has been accepting, if not always enthusiastic, of the many twists and turns of my life thereafter. When the Navy sent me away for months she accepted the role of a single parent, head of household, then packed up and moved when change of duty orders arrived. In military terms, she served "Above and beyond the call of duty". Around Navy communities one would see this bumper sticker: "Navy Wife, Toughest Job in the Navy".

"We cannot give our children what we do not have."

Anon.

chapter six
SCHOOL DISASTER

You probably never realized how badly my public school education got screwed up or what a profound effect that had on my self-image as a below average student with a below-average intellect.

On September 3, 1934, I entered the first grade of Wilder School and I loved it! I was five years old and for three years I had watched Jim with envy as he boarded the school bus every morning and returned each afternoon with books, papers and talk of teachers and blackboards and classes. As he and Mom looked at his papers and read his books, I stuck my face into the activity, soaking up all the excitement. So when it was finally my turn I hit the ground running.

It was a day to remember! I boarded the old black, wood bus with orange lettering and headed for Wilder, a town of a few hundred residents, one general store that also served as the post office, a creamery, gas station, grain elevator and the school, a two-story building constructed of dark colored brick. It housed all twelve grades in three classrooms, each containing four grades with one teacher teaching all subjects to all four grades. There was no kindergarten, no pre-K. "My room" was home to grades one through four, each grade seated alphabetically in its column, front to back. There were just four pupils in first grade, three other boys and me. Last alphabetically, I was assigned the last seat at the back of the room. I was usually the last called upon to recite, read or write on the blackboard. (I was soon to learn that with that last name I would be called upon last for years in many venues, and what psychological effects this had I will leave to the psychologists.) But this spot had its advantages; I could see the entire room, watching and listening to the lessons of the upper three grades as well as our own. At the end of each lesson we were given an assignment to work on at our desks while the teacher began teaching another grade. I was usually able to finish the assignment quickly and then was free to go to the "library", a few dozen books shelved in pastel-painted orange crates located in a back corner of the room. It was here that my life-long love of reading was born and nourished. Books provided an endless source of knowledge and entertainment. But I also loved arithmetic, geography and I retained much of what I overheard that was being taught to the upper classes. , I later discovered that his voracious appetite and natural ability for learning, was typical for six to eight-year olds as demonstrated in bi-lingual families where children grow up mastering two languages, switching effortlessly from one to the other with nary a lesson.

At home I had learned my ABCs and could print my name in block letters but handwriting in script was a challenge. My farm boy hands calloused from pitchfork and shovel now rebelled at the "Palmer Method" of cursive writing with its curlicues and even strokes across the page. Art projects produced similar results with library paste all over my hands and clothing, the take-home project was a mess.

Arithmetic came easily. Progressing through the grades

I learned addition in the first grade, mastered subtraction in the second grade, multiplication in the third grade and in the fourth grade I was just beginning to understand the mysteries of division when my parents were called in to confer with the teacher and the school superintendent. They were informed of my excellent progress in all of the subjects, how I finished my work and headed for the library while the other three members of my class were not keeping pace. Looking back, it seems that the reasonable action would be to set the others back a grade until they caught up, but that would cause two big problems for the school. First, it would leave me in a class of one boy and, second, the fathers of two of my classmates were members of the School Board who would not look kindly on setting their sons back. So promoting me to the fifth grade would solve both problems for the school, but it would forever impede my education and my love of school and learning. And the other three classmates never finished high school anyhow.

I suppose that my parents were flattered to be told that I was above average and should be promoted to the fifth grade. My dad had only an eighth grade education and neither parent was versed in the theories of education, so they relied on the school's recommendation. Thus it came to pass that I was promoted to the fifth grade after completing only a few weeks of the fourth grade, leaving the fine points of division, history, science and geography unlearned.

Fifth grade was located in another class room that also included grades six, seven and eight. The other fifth grade students had advanced six weeks into their studies, working fractions in arithmetic while I had not yet mastered division and, of course I missed the basic introduction to fractions. The teacher had three other grades to teach and several subjects for each grade, leaving no time for tutoring me or any special attention. I eventually mastered fractions and decimals, but to this day algebra problems are like looking at Egyptian hieroglyphics. History class created the same frustration as arithmetic; the class had covered a few hundred years where one age and event flowed into the next and I was plunged midway into the semester's studies without a clue of what had gone before. This floundering soon killed the motivation and excitement I had for books and school. I had moved from the brightest student in the class to the dumbest, consistently failing tests and collecting D's and F's on my report card that reflected both my lack of academic progress and social skills. Completely frustrated, I tried to compensate by playing the class clown, the wise guy, making wisecracks in lieu of correct answers during oral quizzes.

If one's tenth birthday fell within January 1 to December 1, he was enrolled in the same class and that made nearly a year's difference between the oldest and youngest in any given class. A November birthday made me the youngest in my fourth grade class; now with the unexpected promotion I was nearly two years younger than some of my fifth grade classmates and definitely a "baby" to the other three grades in the room. While my clown act amused others in the room and got me some attention, I kept falling further behind, completely losing my love of learning and my self-image of a good student. So it came as no surprise to anyone that I failed the fifth grade and had to repeat it, still retaining little of the content. I remember little of that year or the sixth grade where I was still nearly two years younger than some of my classmates and both academically unprepared and socially undeveloped to keep pace. I do remember making good friends such as Leroy, continuing to develop an interest in girls but generally tuning out all things academic. My parents must have been dismayed at the state of my education, but at some financial sacrifice arranged for me to enroll in seventh grade at Windom Junior High School located in the next county, another situation for which I was academically unprepared, unmotivated and tossed into a social milieu where the other students had been together for six years and had progressed academically in an orderly fashion. They were prepared and eager to begin junior high. Their six-year friendships, shared experiences and social groups were well established. I was definitely an outsider.

These years were the 1930s; no school counselors, teachers were teaching multiple subjects to multiple grades and my parents, uneducated, were unable to imagine another option. I spent the next year and a half in a daze, making a few friends, feeling left out of the social structure and completely unmotivated and unprepared to understand the course of study. Homework assignments were trumped by chores on the farm. The one bright spot in my education at this time was a continued love of reading as previously noted. I read all the farm magazines, back issues of Readers' Digest and Good Housekeeping that had been passed down from more affluent relatives. "Old Yeller" and "Scudda Ho, Scudda Hay" were both serialized in a farm journal as well as "Lassie Come Home". Those stories plus the romantic stories in women's magazines fed my hunger for reading.

About six months into the eighth grade, about a year and a half in the Windom school, Dad had an opportunity to rent a much larger farm located about twenty miles north of Windom. He saw this as a way to get ahead financially and climb out of the depths of the Great Depression. For me it meant another change of schools, this time to a one-room country school with one teacher for all grades. There was no one enrolled in the eighth grade so the teacher was obliged to take on not only another student, but another entire course of study for the three months remaining in the school year. Since I was already floundering from a junior high school, I totally "turned off and tuned out". The lessons sounded like a foreign language. The textbooks were different, there was no one in the class to help me and the teacher of several grades and numerous subjects had no time to tutor me. Jim, the crown prince, remained with friends in Windom to complete his senior year in school and play in the band, so I was now responsible for some of his chores on the farm.

Somehow at the end of the year I was awarded a certificate of completion and then in the fall, enrolled in Comfrey High

School's ninth grade. Here again I, an outsider, joined an established community of students who had been together for eight years, had equal academic preparation. They were "on the same page", as we now say. The next year and a half of school is a blur. I made a couple of close friends, rode the school bus to and from school, but my love of learning had all but vanished.

I was fourteen years old and in the depth of an undiagnosed adolescent crisis. Neither I nor my parents were familiar with that term or the angst it connoted. I had lost all interest in school, going through the motions, shuffling through classes. At home I performed a man's work while Jim played his trombone in Windom. We had thirty dairy cows to milk, feed and clean up after. We had horses to groom, to feed, to harness and work hauling grain, feed and manure. We had hogs to feed and breed and birth and nurse in Minnesota winters.

There were some appealing aspects of life on the farm. A creek ran through the property, a venue for ice skating in winter, fishing and skinny-dipping in summer. Working with the animals touched something deep within my being, a connection to life in many manifestations. Alone in the fields and hikes along the creek I tried to peer into the future, consider my life's work. Farming was hard work but it had its rewards; watching the crops grow from seed to harvest, birthing of calves, pigs, foals and lams, and nursing them and nurturing them brought deep satisfaction. The magic the seasons with the windstorms and hail that destroyed the crops, epidemics that wiped out the lives of swine and the blizzards challenging our ability to carry on the daily routines.

Now into my teens I began to look forward, thinking about the kind of life that lay ahead. Farming was hard work, but it had its advantages. Watching the crops growing from seed to harvest, birthing of calves, pigs, foals and lambs and nursing them and nurturing them created a satisfying sense of accomplishment. Being a part of nature, experiencing the turn of the seasons, including the hardships of blizzards, hail and drought brought a sense of meaning and purpose to my young life. Dad had quit school after eighth grade to work on his dad's farm, so one day I announced to him that I was through with school and ready to work full time at farming. He exploded! "You are going to finish high school if I have to drive you through with a club!" That left little room for discussion of my plan. Later I realized how much he had regretted dropping out, and in retrospect, his ultimatum was the best thing that could have happened to me at that moment.

The next chapter in my so-called education began when Dad decided that it was time again to move, this time back closer to Windom where I was once more enrolled in Windom High School, six months into the tenth grade. Here I experienced again the trauma of re-entering an established community, the same one I had left two years previously, with a common history of orderly progression through the classes. . Two thirds of the school year was over and the curriculum completely foreign to the one I had just left. I remembered many of my classmates from junior high, but friendships and cliques that had formed over the years were slow to admit "the new kid". Teachers were sympathetic, but had little time for tutoring or special attention to my situation. I was still a farm boy, so when classes were over I boarded the yellow school bus and went home to several hours of chores. Farm work is always there. Most of the town kids practiced football, basketball, band, or just socialized at the local soda fountain, or went ice skating on the river. The brainy ones did homework, worked on extra credit projects and took music lessons. I fed animals, milked cows, and cleaned up after the entire menagerie.

By my senior year, Jim of course had graduated and was working on the farm so I successfully pleaded to play on the football team. Mom and Dad arranged for me to stay with a friend from church five nights a week, returning home for the week-end of chores after Friday's game. I didn't get to play much since the other guys had years of experience, but here I felt accepted and enjoyed the camaraderie of the daily practice and suiting up for the games and socializing with team mates in the locker rooms.

None of this advanced my academic standing; nonetheless I was still able to graduate with a "C" average, nothing to brag about, but still better than half of the class. My transcript would not enhance an application for college.

"My teen age years were like a never ending tooth ache."
Anton Chekhov

chapter seven
BUMBLING THROUGH
ADOLESCENCE

Dad and Mom, I do not remember hearing the term "teen-ager"; it may not have yet entered the English language in 1941. If "adolescence" was in use I did not hear it in your vocabulary, nor in mine. Dr. Spock had not written his "common sense" book of child care based on new psychological principles and common sense. So together we stumbled into the sea of my teenage trauma without chart or compass, doing what everyone else was doing, flying by the seats of our pants.

I turned thirteen on November 26, 1941. America had begun to recover from the Great Depression and even the Weir family's fortunes were beginning to improve. In 1937 Dad had purchased a new Chevy sedan, later a new John Deere tractor and now I was even sporting some store-bought clothes of my own. We had taken a family vacation to northern Minnesota seeing the iron mines, the port of Duluth and the beautiful North Shore Drive. The following year we took a second trip, this time to the Black Hills of South Dakota to view the Badlands, to watch the busts of Presidents taking shape on Mt. Rushmore and driving scenic byways through the Hills.

Then, just eleven days after my thirteenth birthday, the Japanese bombed Pearl Harbor, catching our armed forces completely off guard. The attack was devastating, a story that has been retold too many times to repeat here. Many of our finest warships were sunk. The entire country was stunned. Congress and President Roosevelt immediately declared war on Japan, Germany and their allies. The devastation to our navy and other military installations and equipment and the threat of further attacks caused the whole country to be transformed into a massive production machine to support the war effort. Automobile factories were converted to produce tanks, jeeps and other military vehicles. Shipyards were expanded to construct warships, troop ships and cargo vessels. Thousands of able bodied men were drafted or enlisted in the army, navy, marines or air force. Women were working in shipyards, airplane factories and other jobs vacated by men now serving in uniform. It seemed that everyone's life was changed overnight. We all knew someone in uniform. Houses displayed service flags in front windows with a blue star for every man or woman in service and a gold star for each person killed in action. Hollywood movie stars appeared at rallies to sell War Bonds to finance the war effort. Gasoline was rationed as well as many foodstuffs such as sugar and meat since America was shipping food and supplies to our allies in Europe. A national speed limit of 35 MPH was imposed to conserve gasoline. German submarines prowled the Atlantic sea lanes, sinking our ships laden with food, war materials, and thousands of American troops on their way to Great Britain, our ally already devastated by the war. Our country was infused with a spirit of patriotism and fear of our enemies.

It was in this world of turbulence, preoccupied with the war that I stumbled into adolescence. My coming of age was marked with the usual angst of acne, a changing voice, the appearance of body hair and raging hormones. These two concerns, the war and my hormones, eclipsed any interest in the disaster of my public schooling previously related. I bumbled from one class to another, year after year. I was too young to enter the service but like most boys I was still fascinated with all things military. I pored over recruiting material from the Navy, imagining myself in uniform. I built model warplanes from balsa wood kits, suspending them from the ceiling of my bedroom. We watched the combat action in movie newsreels that stirred our patriotic fever. Newspapers carried news of battle in places like Leyte Gulf, Saipan, Corregidor, Tarawa, Iwo Jima and Okinawa. In Europe the war was being fought in faraway places with strange names: Tobruk in North Africa, then Sicily, Italy, St. Lo, and Omaha Beach. .

Day by day, at the cost of thousands of lives on both sides, the allied forces drove back the axis forces of Italy and Germany. D-Day, the massive and costly invasion of Europe marked the beginning of the end. These were battles that were reported daily in the newspapers, on newsreels and radio, and would be told in military history books for generations to come. One night I had a vivid dream of arriving home from the service, wearing a blue uniform adorned with gold braid and medals of valor, sitting astride a white horse from a hilltop overlooking the farm. (Psychologists of the world, shrink that!)

Early in my senior year of high school I turned seventeen. Some of my classmates secured their parents' permission to leave school and enlist in one of the armed services. Mother and Dad were having no part of that even though the war had ended dramatically with the explosion of two atom bombs on Japan. Jim had graduated in 1943 and had been given a deferment from the draft as an essential provider of food for both the armed forces and our war-torn allies whose lands had been devastated by combat. Meanwhile my interest in the Navy continued to grow. In the spring of 1946 as my graduation approached, Jim was reclassified 1-A, available for military service. Even though the war had ended earlier when Japan and Germany had surrendered unconditionally, the draft board none the less was still taking men to replace the combat veterans who were now being rapidly discharged.

Our county's pool of eligible candidates for military service was nearly exhausted. I was still seventeen, ineligible for draft but the local draft board saw me (soon to finish high school) as man to replace my brother on the farm. So it came to pass in the spring of 1946 Jim was drafted for military service. During the reporting process he asked for and was selected for the Navy's quota of that month. He passed the physical and was sent to San Diego, California for boot camp. I do not remember that my future was ever discussed, but it was tacitly understood that upon graduation I would remain on the farm working with Dad. Jim had once again been first in uniform, usurping my dreams of joining the Navy. During these war years, adolescent years, I struggled to come of age, to establish my identity, my place in the world, in the community, in the family and to find my life's work. My interest in the Navy was now somewhat dampened as Jim...as usual...had already done that and I would have no part of continuing to live in his shadow. No more "me too". The Middle Child was seeking his own identity, his own path, blazing a new trail. These concerns were discussed only in my head as I had learned long ago that my opinions and ideas were quickly ridiculed or vetoed. "Who do you think you are anyhow? "Shut up, Goofus!"

I was fourteen years old when our church had installed a new minister and I became friends with the preacher's son, two years younger than me. He would visit the farm for a few days and I was allowed to spend a few days with his family, sometimes traveling with them when they went to church meetings and out of town camps. Here I was exposed to my first non-farm lifestyle. The minister arose daily at a reasonable hour, enjoyed a leisurely breakfast with his family, retired to his study to read and prepare sermons (awesomely referred to as sermonizing) then often have a nap. After lunch he would dress in suit and tie and make pastoral visits to the hospital, drop in on the Ladies' Missionary Society meeting and come home to afternoon tea. His evenings were spent at various meetings and classes. He once asked me if I had considered the ministry as my life's vocation. Our family was nominally religious, regular church and Sunday school goers, and we recited grace before meals. Dad was named an Elder, Mother was active in the Women's Missionary Society and Jim sang in the choir, but I do not recall any talk of religion or personal faith at home. We talked "church" but not religion. We talked about getting the chores done and getting cleaned up for church and Sunday school. The ministry was considered a "holy calling", a vocation set apart from the mundane world of farmers and we were farmers.

The Reverend followed up his earlier question about the ministry by interesting me in attending a church summer camp for teens, two weeks at a lakefront campground in northern Minnesota. I would be awarded a full scholarship to the camp if I would memorize the 120 questions and answers of the Shorter Catechism. I jumped at the chance and took the little 3" x 4" paper bound catechism and began to commit it to memory. I carried it in the pocket of my blue chambray work shirt as I worked in the fields, reciting answer after answer. Memorization seemed to come easily for me and in a few weeks the minister gave me an oral test and I recited the answers to all 120 questions. I realized there that I had a natural capacity for memorization and to this day can recite numerous Psalms, poems, and chapters of Scripture learned seventy-five years ago in first grade.

The two week camp proved to be a bright interlude in my teen years, and it would prove to be a significant influence in my life. Early morning swims in the lake, three nutritious meals daily, inspirational speakers, Bible study classes, campfires, sing-alongs of gospel hymns and choruses were shaping my life in significant ways. And no chores! No damned chores! At camp I was asked again to listen for God's guidance in the choice of a vocation, of a life work. Missionaries told of their work in faraway lands. Seminary students related their experiences in studying for the ministry and teachers at mission schools spoke of their work with Native Americans. "Quiet times" were scheduled where we were encouraged to find a solitary place to contemplate our lives, to pray and listen for God's direction for our lives.

To a farm kid like me this routine held a lot more appeal than milking cows at dawn, cleaning the barns and driving a tractor in the fields all day. Farming required an endless battle against the plagues of cockleburs, ragweed, thistles and grasshoppers. I had seen Dad and other farmers watch helplessly as disease killed their hogs, cattle and poultry. Hail, drought, windstorms and early freezes wiped out half a year's labor in fields of corn and other grains, and with it, the hope of a decent income. Tilling the soil brought rocks and stones to the surface, debris deposited by some melting prehistoric glacier and left them for us to gather haul to some barren, unbillable and remote corner. I remember also we had to leave the Sunday afternoon church picnic early to milk cows and gather dried corn cobs in the pig pens to heat wash-water for Monday's laundry while my city friends continued to play ball and get seconds of ice-cream at the picnic.

Although I loved the outdoor life that the farm provided, hiking through the pastures, fishing, hunting and observing wildlife, I knew there must be a life for me that was not tied to the demands and risks of diversified farming. I began looking at the work and lives of the non-farmers in our community, gas station operators, grocers, retail stores, and yes, even my barber. I mentally tried on these roles imagining how they felt, how my life might be in one of these occupations. In my senior year of high school I had become friends with the son of the bank president. I was invited to accompany his family on a trip to Minneapolis and attend both the State High School Basketball Tournament and the Ice Follies. On this trip I discovered a way of life I had not dared to dream. I was taken to lunch at a fancy restaurant where we were served on linen table cloths and with sterling silverware and coffee service. We had tickets for choice seats at the Follies and the games. We stayed at a relative's luxurious home where I was treated as one of the family. Wow, I thought, me, Goofus, eating with silver and linen tablecloths and treated like the banker's son. Wow!

These experiences reinforced my unconscious need to get out of town, get out of the role of #2 son, to kick over the traces, to explore the world and find a life and an identity that was uniquely mine. The middle child was restless and determined to make his own way. I had tentatively settled on the ministry, a path where no Weir had gone before. I did not hear the voice of God from heaven. I had no dramatic, emotional experience. I had no vision of saving the souls of the heathen. It was a pragmatic reasoned decision that would provide the recognition and the status and lifestyle that I saw in the preacher and the banker and their families. It has been said that God sometimes uses our basest motives to build His kingdom. Amen.

chapter eight
COLLEGE

Remember the summer of 1946? None of us knew much about college, how to apply, what academic standards would be required and, most of all, how academically unprepared I was, what an unlikely scholar. But we forged ahead, you proud to have a son studying for the ministry, me happy to be the center of attention, happy to leave the farm, leave the little brother role and make my own life.

The war had been over for a year, and just at the time Jim completed his basic training, the war department announced that all reserves and draftees were to be released from duty and sent home at the earliest possible date. There was great joy throughout the country that the enemies surrendered, the war was over and that sons and fathers and brothers would soon be reunited with their families. When Jim was released shortly after completing boot camp with a total of 87 days of active duty, I announced that I wanted to go to college.

It was now late July and the college year began the day after Labor Day. No one in our family had ever gone to college so we didn't know how to proceed. We relied on the advice of our minister who predictably recommended his alma mater, University of Dubuque College and Seminary in Dubuque, Iowa, some 350 miles from home. Ordination in the Presbyterian Church required four years of undergraduate study earning a bachelor degree, followed by three years of theological seminary. There were many colleges closer to home and probably less expensive and just as good, but we knew nothing about them and time was short. There was no second opinion and no guidance counselor. The college advised us that enrollments were filling rapidly with thousands of veterans returning to take advantage of the GI Bill of Rights legislation that offered them a free college education. Neither Mom or Dad questioned my choice and quietly did all that was required to support me. We scrambled to get through the application process, transcript of high school grades, and letters of recommendation. Both parents were caught up in the process, saying little of their feelings, but meeting every deadline, checking off every requirement. The preacher announced my plans during Sunday services, placing a feather in his hat for recruiting a soldier in God's army. We also had to buy some suitable clothing and dormitory furnishings. Mother assembled bedding, towels, luggage plus a laundry case to send my dirty clothes and bedding home for her to wash, press and return. My letter of acceptance arrived stating that the campus dormitories were filled, but that a suitable off-campus room nearby had been reserved for me. I said goodbye to Jim, Emmy and Shep as Dad, Mom and I piled into the now-aging '37 Chevy and set out for Dubuque, the farthest from home I had ever travelled.

The room that the college had arranged for me was in the home of the Rev. and Mrs. M. M. Murrell, located about three blocks from the campus. It was a two story brick home where I shared a room with a Navy veteran registered as a pre-dental student majoring in the sciences. Another room was assigned to two other ministerial students plus a room in the loft housing the Murrell's son, also a vet. That made five college students plus the two aging Murrells in a house with one bathroom! We unloaded my meager possessions, and then Dad drove us the three blocks to the campus where we said our tearful goodbyes. I was "at college". I knew no one but I knew it was dinner time and recognized Peters Commons, the dining hall, from a picture in the college catalog. I fell in line with several hundred others; each seemed to be chatting excitedly with friends. I moved in silence through the cafeteria line and through the meal.

No student of higher education ever arrived at college with less aptitude or more poorly prepared than I. A C-minus high school transcript, non-existent study habits and the self-image of a poor student engendered by the debacle of my public school experience did not bode well for college studies. I had no mentor, no scholarly model and no real passion for learning. Here I was suddenly thrust into a class that was made up of valedictorians and honor students from many Midwestern high schools. Many were from families where parents and siblings were college-educated so they arrived with scholarly models, established study habits and sources of mentoring and motivation. The war veterans, all several years older, were focused on studies and careers, wise in the ways of the adult world. Some were married.

Not only was I academically unprepared, I had been unknowingly protected from the ways of the world by the small town, puritanical constraints, including some basic facts of life. I had never heard the word "circumcision". Of course I had been in group showers after gym classes and football practice, noticing that some guys were laid out differently than others, but I assumed that it was the way we were born, like blue eyes or brown, red hair or blonde. It was only reading an assignment in Old Testament that I came across Genesis 17:10, "Every man child among you shall be circumcised, and you shall circumcise the flesh of your foreskin; and it shall be a token of the covenant between me and you." Hmmm! A new word! So to the new and as yet unopened dictionary: "circumcision: to cut off the foreskin of a male". O.K. next: "foreskin: the fold of skin that covers the glans of the penis". Hmmm: "Glans: a conical vascular body forming the extremity of the penis". So that's it! Not all education occurs in the classroom. I was born on a cold a Minnesota house, and the family doctor was not about to perform any optional surgery on me. So that's it! The other guys were born in a hospital and circumcised in a sterile operating room.

Reading further in Genesis I would learn of Lot's daughters getting their father drunk on wine so they could get pregnant with him and also about a guy name Onan whose story reads: "And Judah said unto Onan (his son) Go in unto thy slain brother's wife and marry her, and raise up seed to thy brother …..and Onan knew that the seed should not be his; and it came to pass when he went in unto his brother's wife that he spilled it on the ground, lest he should give seed to his brother. And the thing that he did displeased the Lord, wherefore he slew him also." I never heard that one at home or in First Presbyterian Church of Windom!.

Growing up on the farm I was well acquainted with, and witness to, the breeding of cows, horses, hogs and sheep. Yes, chickens too. I had midwifed the birth of many of these animals. There were never any formal lessons or explanations or discussions, it was simply learn by observation and keep your mouth shut. Sexual relations between men and women were never mentioned either at home or church or classroom. They were the subject of jokes and innuendos, references to easy women related in vernacular terms in the locker room or barber shop. Unfortunately, I had never heard the word "homosexual" and was unprepared for the day when I was first approached, an event I relate in a later chapter. I had no clue that some men and women were physically, sexually attracted to people of their own gender.

My roommate was a pre-dental school student, highly motivated and majoring in the physical sciences. He was a friendly fellow but wanted to be accepted in the best dental schools so he spent little time with chit-chat and lots of time with the books. His three years of military service had taught him self-reliance and discipline.

As an announced pre-theological student (everyone said "pre-the", long e, rhymes with three), I was assigned to Dr.

Kenneth Smith, Ph.D. professor of Greek and New Testament as my "counselor". He helped me complete my class schedule, a boilerplate for pre-thes, to meet the first requirements for a bachelor's degree four years hence. "One science credit: biology, check! One English credit: Rhetoric 101, check! One foreign language: Greek I: check! One history credit: Early American history (oops, that class filled) 19th Century Europe: check! Physical education: Gym 101: check! Social Studies: Sociology 101: check! Good bye and good luck. Next!" That was my "counseling".

I had no interest in biology. Memorizing parts of bugs, phylum, class, and order was pure boredom. I would have preferred chemistry, but the "big people" know best, so I kept quiet. I had no idea what sociology was, and really no interest in finding out. And how could I learn the no-longer-spoken Koine Greek grammar when I didn't understand the rules of English grammar. (Years later Greek served to solve crossword puzzles; e.g. "eleventh letter of the Greek alphabet, *lambda*). My "counseling" lasted about six minutes and I left registration with a schedule of classes stapled to a list of textbooks to purchase and feeling as if I had been spit out of a machine.

My recollections of my freshman year are a blur of classrooms, teachers, books, assignments. In high school, homework or study outside of the class had been preempted by the farm chores, so here at college instead studying, I worked part time in the dining room washing dishes and later, just hanging out with other farm boys and pre-thes. I shuffled in and out of classrooms, sitting invisibly in the back row with Walters, Williams and Wright.

There were however, two faculty members who took special interest in me and who saved my academic life from complete disaster. Ms. Vivian Newport taught English Composition 101 and on the first day of class assigned us to write a three page essay. Me? Write an essay? Voices from the past ranted in my mind. "Goofus! Goofus! Who do you think you are, somebody special?" Nonetheless I managed to cover three pages with my crabbed scrawl. After reading that first pathetic assault on the English language, Ms. Newport kept me after class and said in substance: "Young man, if you aspire to be a minister, you must master the English language, both written and spoken. That mastery begins in this class. It begins now and I am here to teach you. You are to re-write this paper. You will see that I have covered the page with corrections, suggestions and questions. The content is good. The ideas are fine, but you need to work on the expression, the clarity of each sentence. Do not let my corrections discourage you. You have great potential and a great opportunity to develop it. Now go and begin."

Week after week the process continued with her patience, suggestions, corrections, rewrites and encouragement. I learned many of the basics of grammar and syntax in this class and the following year I enrolled in Ms. Newport's elective creative writing class where my writing developed further under her coaching. I was stunned when she chose one of my first articles to read before the class, pointing out the colorful use of language. She did more for my self-confidence and esteem in that moment than I had experienced in a lifetime. As longtime avid reader I had acquired an innate sense of how sentences were constructed and how they flowed from one into another and where to make paragraph breaks, and Ms. Newport's coaching and tutoring nourished both my tender ego and my writing skills.

The second person to express a personal interest in my education and development was Stanley Newcomb, Professor of Speech and Drama who was addressed throughout the campus simply as "Prof". He was the epitome of tough love, stopping me in the middle of a speech to correct, suggest, guide and make me repeat. He taught me to vary the pitch, tone, and timbre of my voice and the use of the dramatic pause. I took most of his classes in college and several more later in seminary. I studied debate, interpretive reading and drama. He also hired me as stage manager of the campus' Little Theater, a student aid job that paid fifty cents an hour building sets for plays and wardrobes for costumes plus janitorial and general handyman projects. Then he hired me to do some gardening at his home. Prof's mentoring and modeling would add more to my effectiveness as a preacher than all the Greek syntax in Greece

Under the tutelage of these two dedicated teachers, these mentors, my college education began to move forward, but the report cards in my other subjects reconfirmed that I was Goofus, the farmer, nobody special, not a student. I was literally sleep-walking through college, going through the motions. I enjoyed new friendships, attending chapel services, vespers and other religious activities and the freedom from farm chores, but I spent a lot of free time just "goofing off" or "hanging out" and smoking.. Smoking had been forbidden at home, but I had sneaked a smoke on every opportunity. Smoking was considered sophisticated. It seemed that every movie star acted with a cigarette in hand. Gifts for servicemen overseas usually contained a carton of "Luckies", "Camels" or "Chesterfields". Airlines distributed free samples of cigarettes to their passengers. A high percentage of the GI students had picked up the habit in the service and I quickly picked up the habit in college.

I had never tasted alcohol nor did I like the smell of it. One evening after report cards had come out with my very poor grades, and a girlfriend had left me for a football star, I was feeling "down in the dumps" .A few of my dorm mates said they had just the cure for me and took me to a nearby bar and introduced me to whiskey sours. They tasted like lemonade with a kick and I consumed an estimated ten of these seamlessly harmless quaffs before we left and started walking back to the dorm. Suddenly I was seriously ill, throwing up everything I had eaten or drunk in the past 24 hours. My friends literally carried me back to the dorm where I slept it off and awoke with an enormous headache and a body that felt like it had been beaten.

If I was academically unprepared for college I was equally unprepared for a self-directed life. Looking back I think of how much I could have profited from a mentor, a coach, and a counselor. Why at the end of my first semester didn't someone... counselor...advisor...look at my report card and pull me out of Greek? Examine my aptitude for college? For ministry? Why did not someone assign me to mandatory and supervised study hours, assign a senior as my tutor? Why did not Presbytery's "Committee on Oversight of Candidates" enforce some standards? What could I have done with the two years wasted on Greek grammar? I did not verbalize these questions, but just plodded along, muddling through each day as it arrived. One of those days, mulling my situation while on a solitary walk, I asked God or Somebody to give me a visible sign that my life was on the right path. Of course there was no sign and I continued going through the motions of college classes.

chapter nine
UNDER CARE

Dad, do you remember driving me to Pipestone for the Presbytery meeting where I stood for oral examinations? You must have been very proud, hearing the "fathers and brethren" quiz me on matters theological and ecclesiastical. That was the year you bought me a twelve year old 1935 Dodge for my summer field work. Thank you!

The Presbyterian Church takes its name from the Greek word, presbyter, that translates "elder". Each local congregation is governed by the Session, comprised of one teaching elder, the minister, who serves as moderator, and several ruling elders, ordained laypersons who are not theologically trained, but elected and ordained on the basis of their character and demonstrated piety. The session manages the spiritual life of the church, dispenses the sacraments and approves the program of worship, music and education of all ages. The real power and authority in the Presbyterian Church is vested in the Presbytery, all the ordained ministers and a representative number of ruling elders within a fixed geographical area. The Presbytery owns the property of each congregation, has the power to ordain ministers, must approve the hiring and departure of ministers in each of the member churches and supervise the training and education of "candidates" for the ministry. The supervision of candidates begins with a formal procedure known as the candidates "Being Taken Under the Care of Presbytery. At some point during my college years I was formally questioned regarding my spiritual experiences, my motivation in seeking "Care" and was "Taken Under the Care of Mankato Presbytery" a cluster of Presbyterian churches in southwestern Minnesota. I reported my progress to their "Committee on Oversight" on a regular schedule including my academic report cards.

During my senior year in college I was advised that during the coming summer months between college and seminary I would be "filling the pulpit" of the Presbyterian Church at Rushmore, MN, a rural village some forty-five miles from home. This was a "Sunday only" assignment, so I would still be working for Dad on the farm during the week. My title would be, "temporary supply", which meant conducting Sunday worship and preaching every Sunday during my "vacation". I was not ordained so I could not administer the sacraments of baptism and the Lord's Supper, could not perform marriages nor moderate the Session. A minister from a nearby town was designated as the Moderator and was responsible for those functions. Dad located and purchased a 1935 Dodge sedan, the most basic of basic means of transportation for the weekly commute. I remember that the interior had been home-reupholstered in a red, flocked floral pattern. It functioned well. In fact I would drive it back to Dubuque at summer's end. The church provided a modest weekly stipend for my services.

It was with fear and trembling that I approached these duties. I had no formal training in sermon preparation. I knew the "order of worship" from memory, having attended a Presbyterian Church weekly my entire life. I knew all the words of all the verses to most of the hymns. I had years of Bible study, but I had not a clue about translating this experience into sermon to be preached to these life-long Presbyterians. My "salvation" was found in a book of sermons that I received as a college graduation gift. I memorized, stole, cribbed, borrowed and plagiarized every word of that book, thereby giving the humble, pious and patient members of Rushmore much more than my untrained and befuddled mind could ever have provided. Prof. Newcomb's classes in speech and drama had given me the confidence to deliver these purloined lessons with poise and conviction. The good folks of Rushmore seemed sincerely pleased to have my services, and the experience increased my confidence that, just perhaps, my vocation was well-chosen, that I could learn to do this work and really be of service, comfort and inspiration to future congregations. I thrived on the adulation of the congregation. At summer's end they presented me with a cash gift, a bonus if you will, to help with the tuition at the seminary.

chapter ten
SEMINARY

Dad, I'm sure I have never promptly thanked you for the Dodge and later the Ford, and then the Kaiser, not to mention the tuition, room, board and more. The cars were necessary to carry out the fieldwork, the week-end preaching in various churches. Thank you!

College had been an academic struggle but it was nothing compared to what lay ahead in seminary; that would require a whole new level of intellectual labor. University of Dubuque Theological Seminary was a one hundred year old institution originally named The German Theological School of the Northwest. In 1852 Iowa was still considered the northwest. At its founding the school consisted of a single clergyman named Adrian Van Vliet who took several young men under his personal tutelage to prepare them for the ministry. The program grew to include other ministers preparing other young men, always in the German language to preach in German to first generation German Presbyterians that populated eastern Iowa. Over the years the formal theological seminary evolved, and later the college of liberal arts was formed. Gradually the population around the area had diversified; English became the established language in the public schools and in the government, and the exclusively German speaking population was dying off. A few churches still worshipped in both German and English, but those were soon to vanish.

The seminary had recently hired a new dean, Dr. Elwyn Smith, a freshly minted Ph.D. out of Yale University. He had been chosen for and charged with raising the academic standards to be on a par with the other Presbyterian seminaries in Princeton, Pittsburgh, Chicago , and San Francisco.

Dean Smith took his mandate seriously, raised the academic standards to graduate level, hired faculty with excellent intellectual credentials, introduced curriculum that reflected 20th century thought and practices designed to develop clergy who could relate the gospel to a new, post-World War II generation.

In my senior year at the college I had casually submitted an application for admission to the seminary, a short walk across the quadrangle on the same campus. It was not many weeks later that Dean Smith summoned me to his office for the admissions interview. When I entered his office I was wordlessly motioned to a seat while he studied what appeared to be my college transcript and other application documents. He finally looked up and greeted me: "Weir, this is a disgraceful record. What makes you think that you are capable of graduate work?" I was stunned! Speechless! I'm sure I blushed. No one had ever spoken to me like that. I felt like Daniel in the lion's den. After all, was I not "called"! Who could doubt that I was destined, divinely ordained to be enrolled in seminary? I had given no thought that it might be different than coasting through college, sitting through classes, lectures, reading books, and passing tests. If I mumbled some sort of reply to him, I don't remember what it might have been. Probably it was some gibberish about the divine call and the recommendation of others. After allowing me to sweat in silence for a few minutes he announced, "Weir, I am admitting you to this seminary on probation. You have six weeks to show me you can cut the mustard here or you are out on your ear. Is that clear?" No doubt about it, I understood and departed "with my tail between my legs".

The fall of 1950 I was thrust abruptly into the sea of systematic theology, homiletics, New Testament studies in Greek and Old Testament studies in Hebrew, preaching and pastoral care. My textbooks were John Calvin's "The Institutes of the Christian Religion" in two volumes, the catechism of Martin Luther, "Systematic Theology" in two volumes by Paul Tillich, Reinhold Niebuhr's "The Nature and Destiny of Man", "Fear and Trembling" by the Danish philosopher Soren Kierkegaard and "Dogmatiks" by Karl Barth, the darling of the theology professor.

There were studies of the Bible, Old and New Testaments, gospels and epistles, psalms and prophets, Biblical wars and wanderings.

I was bombarded with such concepts as orthodoxy, neo-orthodoxy, existentialism, dialectical theology, infralapsarianism, nihilism, expository preaching, and exegetical preaching. Gone were the true/false, multiple choice, and fill in the blank quizzes. In their place were essays analyzing differing or opposing schools of thought and making a choice to defend one or another.

As I wrestled to understand these ideas and the differences in the thoughts of such intellectuals, for the first time I began to realize that there was no one, single, universal truth subscribed to by the great minds of protestant theology. I found encouragement in the works of Emil Brunner who believed in nature's ability to reveal spiritual truth, and in Paul Tillich who used the term "ground of our being" to describe the nature of God. My youthful and parochial concepts of "The Big Guy in the Sky" who heard and answered our prayers, and who doled out rewards and punishment, were now called into question. The traditional "Reform theology" of John Calvin and John Knox, "fathers" of Presbyterianism, declared the Bible to be the only infallible word of God. Then the professors lectured on the Council of Nicaea where Emperor Constantine brought together the bishops from all over the world, requiring them to speak with one voice, hence, under duress these sixth century theologians hammered out the doctrine of the Trinity arguing whether the Holy Spirit proceeded only from the Son or the Father and the Son.

Studies in preaching explained expository sermons, doctrinal sermons, biographical, textual, and topical sermons, their construction and delivery. The height of this potpourri of academic theology was the extended series of classes given to explain the differences between infralapsarianism and supralapsarianism and why one was orthodox and the other heresy. I didn't understand it then, I don't understand it now, and I don't think it matters.

What is understandable is that I was having second and third thoughts about my "call", about my fitness for ministry, about my ability to complete the courses of study that were mentally drowning me. Maybe it was time to step back, reconsider my path and change direction. Just as importantly I was beginning to see the crumbling of my perceived monolithic religious truth. Learned scholars addressed as "The Reverend Doctor", who had spent decades studying Christian doctrine, differed widely in their understanding of the faith. History of the church related inquisitions, wars, crusades and burning of heretics. To me all of this seemed foreign to the Sermon on the Mount, the Beatitudes, and the music of the Psalms.

It was the critical study of the formation the New Testament and the early history of the Church that raised serious questions about the Bible as the divinely inspired Word of God. Jesus had not organized churches, built marble temples, created bishops who sat on thrones, wore crowns and carried scepters and who claimed to speak alone for God. It was over three hundred years after the life of Christ that Christianity had spread throughout the Roman Empire. With this growth had come variations of the teachings and practices of individual churches; most notable was the doctrine of the trinity, Father, Son and Holy Spirit, the three persons taught in the Scriptures. Roman emperor Constantine, in an effort to solidify his empire, convened a council of bishops with instructions for all churches and bishoprics to speak with one voice for the Church. The council assembled in Ephesus in the year 325 and was attended by over 300 delegates including bishops from Alexandria, Jerusalem, Gaul, Constantinople, and Caesarea to mention a few.

It was this gathering now known as the First Council of Ephesus that the doctrine of the Trinity was hammered out in compromises three centuries after Jesus had visited the world, and is still recited in the mass and liturgical worship around the world.

My first conscious urgings to disbelieve, to "bail out", to break free of the traditions, the expectations of family and other big people came when I sensed a gulf between the biblical teachings of Psalms, prophets and the New Testament Sermon on the Mount, and the theologies being built upon the creeds and catechism of third century clerics coerced by the Roman emperor to advance his political agenda. But my feelings went unexpressed, perhaps suppressed, because, after all, the Big People knew best. "Who do you think you are?" lurked in the background. "Goofus" dared not challenge the learned professors and two thousand years of tradition.

The year was 1951. The Korean War was raging; North Korea had invaded South Korea and American armed forces were sent as the major part of the United Nations force to repel the invasion and restore order. Most of my seminary classmates were veterans of WWII and for which I had been too young. Now he draft board had classified me 4-D, exempt as a theological student, and I was also loathe to follow my brother's brief military service. A new interest in military service and I wondered it was patriotism or an acceptable path out of seminary. My grades were much below average. It was a struggle to keep from totally failing my course of study so I decided to go home on Thanksgiving break, consult my parents and pastor, then enlist in the Army. Perhaps I needed time to mature, to better prepare myself for graduate school. And did I really want to spend my life in a small rural community, or was there something else in my destiny? Lest I lose my nerve and/or let the Big People change my mind I went first to the recruiting office in the courthouse on a Friday morning in November the day after Thanksgiving. There posted on the door: "The Recruiting Officer is in this office every Tuesday and Wednesday from 8:00 a.m. to 4:00 p.m."

Was this an omen? Was this a sign from God? Was I like Jonah fleeing from Nineveh where God had called him to preach? Would I embarrass and shame my parents if I quit seminary? Filled with anxiety, mental and spiritual misgivings, I returned to seminary determined to give it my best shot and let the examinations take their course while keeping all my options open. Once again the fear of the Big People dictated to my underdeveloped ego. I stuffed the inner wisdom that was struggling to express itself.

With a new sense of resolve, and growing used to the routine and the demands of graduate study I moved forward. In addition to the strenuous academics of theology, church history and doctrine more courses in the department of practical theology, practicum or pastoral theology. Administration of the sacraments, parish administration, Presbyterian polity....the judicatories of the church and their powers, rights and duties, the local church's session, Presbytery, synod and General assembly each with numerous duties, committees and commissions were all committed to memory. A course in church music, hymnology, and working with a choir, organist, and soloists to achieve worship experience for the flock. There was a class on the larger mission of the church...evangelistic missions, social actions, disaster relief and contingencies. Much of these subjects were included in "field work", the supervised practice of the above duties in nearby churches.

These churches in nearby areas, mostly rural and too small to support a resident minister, relied upon the seminary to provide part-time ministry. Ordained faculty members would go to these congregations to administer the sacraments of baptism and communion and also critique the student who was preaching that day. The students' field work was supervised and graded jointly by the Chairman of the Practical Theology department and the Chairman of Oversight of my Presbytery.

I felt relatively comfortable in these week-end assignments. All my life I had attended Presbyterian churches. I knew the lives of these rural people and could talk hybrid corn and Holstein cows with any of them. I knew all the responses, the rituals, the hymns, and thanks to Stan Newcomb, I could read the Scriptures with empathy and convey the meaning with authority. But, I approached THE SERMON with fear and trembling. How could I, with so many doubts, so much confusion, inspire the faithful and give hope to the sinners? How was I, "Goofus" of the miserable report cards, to impart wisdom and faith to these rural families with their rock-solid faith? Our professor of preaching advised us that when in doubt of what to preach," Rely on your own personal testimony". Me? With my doubts! Me? With my questions about the creeds and sacraments! Me? With questions about creation theories, the literal interpretation of Biblical Stories? I had avoided even bringing these issues fully to my own consciousness; therefore how was I in position to inspire the faithful.

My personal theology began to take shape as I studied the Bible, the creeds and catechisms of the church and the learned volumes of theology: each writer formed his opinions and beliefs from his own encounter with the Divine whether it was in nature with Thoreau, with an encounter with "Oversoul" (the universal mind or spirit that animates, motivates and is the unifying principle of all living things.) of Emerson or in an ecstatic, solitary moment such as Saul experienced on the road to Damascus. I deduced that God chooses to speak to each of us in our present conditions. Was this what Luther meant writing of "the priesthood of all believers". That God speaks to each of us in the way we best hear and understand? Do I stand with the writers of Scripture, to whom God speaks a message for his purpose and in his time? Does Christianity make great strides in the world when God connects in a special way with one seeker who experiences God's presence and voice in a unique way and that becomes the "word of God" for that time and place?

Fortunately the seminary had a library with many volumes interpreting the Bible, books of exegesis to secure the exact meaning of the words, books of exposition to explain the meaning of the story and its teaching. And, there were books of sermons, many books of sermons, sermons for all occasions from which all of us students cribbed, all plagiarized without a twinge of conscious. Better to feed the flock with someone else's harvest rather than lay before them the weeds of doubt and ignorance that were the best our befuddled brains could produce. The recipients of these "borrowed" gems were patient, kind and generous in their reception of the message and the messenger.

One of the courses in "practical theology", the practice of ministry, was homiletics, "the art of preaching". We studied the lives and sermons of some of the great preachers in the history of the church, discussed them in class and were lectured on the preparation and delivery of the weekly homily. This was followed by "practice preaching" where each of us was required to prepare a sermon and deliver it before the class and the professor. The sermon was then critiqued by both the professor and our fellow students. Most of us approached this project with no small amount of fear and trembling, but enjoyed critiquing the preaching of our friends and fellow students. After class we would gather in the student lounge where we teased and mocked the "preacher of the day".

When my turn came (W still last) I had prepared diligently for several weeks, writing, editing and practicing my sermon. I had seen a well-known preacher who stepped out of the pulpit and moved closer to the people, a move that I thought was very effective. I decided to follow that model to set my preaching apart from that of my classmates. Well it did set me apart...the professor criticized me for that, saying I should stay in the pulpit where I belonged. My fellow student-preachers joined in with great delight and gave me a hard time, mocking me and the prof's criticism. When I later entered the student lounge I was met by a chorus of "Get back in the pulpit! Who do you think you are, wandering around the church like a nomad?"

I tried to better their teasing by shouting: "Yes, I left the box! I actually defied centuries of scared tradition. I committed the sacrilege, the unpardonable sin, I left the box! No matter that I preached the gospel with passion, that people were moved to confess the evil of their ways and came forward to find salvation for their eternal souls. That counted for naught because I left the box. As the hazing continued I countered, "BULLSHIT! This is supposed to be a graduate school and this whole course has been nothing but nit picking, snot blowing, bullshit and serves no good end.

My response to both the prof's nit-picking and my classmate's teasing was to become a theme of my life, the non-conforming middle child kicking over the traces of tradition and authority, blazing his own trail.

I finished the first academic year and the summer of 1951 brought a new experience. I was invited/assigned full time work at the Presbyterian Churches in Kimball and Plankinton, South Dakota for the three summer months. These two villages, each with a population of fewer than 900 were located approximately in the middle of the state and surrounded by flat farmland. A room in the home of a young, working couple was provided for me and a desk in the balcony of the church served as my "Office/Study". On Sundays I preached in the Kimball church at 10:00 a.m. then drove the twenty-five miles due east to preach at 11:30 in Plankinton. The people in each location were kind but reserved. I felt like a foreigner in a foreign land. Kimball had one roadside café where I had lunch nearly every day. Chamberlin, the only town of any size or facilities was twenty-five miles farther west where I often drove for a movie, a meal or just to watch the sun set over the Missouri River.

The weeks crept by with ample time to study and memorize the next Sunday's sermon. Officiating my first funeral stands out as the memorable event of the summer. A large community of Czech farmers lived southwest of town. They were not members of "my church" but they came to me asking me to officiate the funeral of an aged member of their clan, the funeral to be held in the home of a family member. I had the Presbyterian Book of Common Worship containing the order for burial of the dead, complete with scripture lessons, prayers and words of committal. I drove far out in the country, then journeyed down a hot and dusty lane to a farm house where I was formally received at the appointed hour, fed from a bounteous buffet along with fifty or so family, friends and neighbors all dressed in clean but well-worn work clothing.

We proceeded to the living room where the late-departed was laid out. I was given the word to commence. I read the service in solemn tones, made remarks that to my 23 year-old heart seemed appropriate. Not knowing what to do next I began moving towards the exit. The man I perceived to be the leader of the clan called out, "Just a moment, Revener (a widely-used colloquial variation of Reverend) have a seat. Then the "real" funeral began. One after another the elders rose to offer long and elaborate eulogies, much of it in the Czech dialect. After sweating through what seemed like hours in the South Dakota summer heat, the deceased body was reverently carried to a pickup truck and we followed to the cemetery for the committal service.

There, in well-kept burial grounds, literally in the midst of nowhere, and amid the sobs and tears of the mourners, I read the service of committal. Experienced and loving hands lowered the homemade casket into the grave. I drove back to my room with a new appreciation of summer "fieldwork" as part of my theological education.

Apparently the reports of my summer work in South Dakota qualified me for the final phase of practical theology. Shortly after the beginning of my second year of seminary I was assigned to a full weekend of work at the Community Church in Mazomanie, Wisconsin. Seminary classes were conducted four days a week, Tuesday through Friday. After Friday classes I drove the 80 miles to the village of Mazomanie where I was graciously welcomed by the good folks of the church and the village. They provided room and meals in the homes of members. In addition to leading the Sunday worship and preaching I taught Sunday School classes, mentored youth groups, and made such pastoral visits to the sick and shut-ins as needed. I basked in the attention and adulation these people heaped on me. I was invited to meals in their homes, family celebrations of birthdays and graduations. I was taken to plays at the University of Wisconsin and to a Big Ten football game. The entire community bestowed a feeling of unconditional acceptance, embracing me with affection, just the way I was. Suddenly it was the spring of 1953, the final semester of seminary was nearly over and I had not made plans beyond final examinations. I was still unmarried with no immediate prospects to marry. I felt disinclined to serve as the pastor in a Midwestern village church. I was equally disinclined to serve on the staff of a large, urban church. So, I concentrated on preparing for final exams, submitting the required essays and continued the work at Mazomanie. The M.Div. degree that now hangs on the wall of my office proclaims the triumph of hard work, the help of friends and the grace of God.

The final step on the seven year journey to becoming a Presbyterian minister was ordination by the Presbytery of Mankato to whom I had reported regularly over the course of my studies. It included submitting an academic paper on a subject of my choice setting forth my personal beliefs and evidence of academic achievement followed by an oral examination before the assembled "fathers and brethren" assembled in a specially called session. I was questioned about my personal religious experience, my theological orthodoxy, and knowledge of all matters theological and ecclesiastical. The first question from the floor was, "Who is God?" I was prepared for that one; it was the first question in the Shorter Catechism that I had memorized for my scholarship to summer camp while in high school. I recited that answer slowly and thoughtfully, as if coming from the depths of my soul. It was received by several moments of silence. I'm certain that none of the lay delegates and some of the clergy did not recognize the source of "my" answer and those who did would not question it. The questions that followed were fairly innocuous and I answered them with everything I had been taught, all of the catechism answers memorized, the creeds and the pronouncements of professors and books of theology.

There were questions about my spiritual life and my personal piety for which I was not prepared. I still had more doubts than faith, more questions than answers. I remembered that class on preaching when the professor stated that if we didn't know what to preach, we could give our personal testimony. I don't remember my "piety" answers but they must have satisfied the brethren as they suspended the questioning and voted to proceed with the ordination.

In the church of my youth with family and well-wishers assembled, there was much talk of "the first son of the church" sent forth into the world to preach the gospel. The clergy of the presbytery continued with the laying-on of hands, granting me authority to administer the sacraments, preach, and perform weddings and all other rites of the church. At age 24 I was now a peer and could participate in their deliberations and vote in their councils. (Yeah, yeah, get on with it…I need a smoke. Now what?)

Midway through that final semester the seminary was visited by Rear Admiral Stanton Salisbury, Chief of Navy Chaplains. He was a Presbyterian clergyman and he was recruiting chaplains for active duty. I requested an interview in which he reminded me that I was still single, had enjoyed a theological deferment from military service throughout my college and seminary years, and that I appeared to be an ideal candidate for the chaplaincy. He likewise related the benefits of regular pay and allowances without relying on a church's budget or renegotiating my salary each year, the great medical and retirement benefits, and most appealing to me, the opportunity to travel. It felt to me like a good fit so I filled out the application forms, and took the train to Chicago to interview with the District Chaplain of the Ninth Naval District at Great Lakes Naval Training Center. A few weeks I received a telegram ordering me to report to the recruiting office in Minneapolis for a physical examination, to be sworn in and to proceed to the Navy Chaplain School in Newport, Rhode Island for eight weeks of training followed by assignment to a permanent duty station. At last I would be in a blue uniform with gold trim, sans white horse, and by god that would show them I was somebody! This would be not so much a noble calling as an escape from the ecclesiastical and community constraints that had long chaffed my spirit.

chapter eleven
IN THE NAVY NOW

Twenty-four years old, two academic degrees in my pocket, a commission as Lieutenant Junior Grade in the United States Navy and a new 1953 Chevy! I thought I had arrived, that I was finally Somebody with a capital S. The Navy sent orders for me to report to the chaplain school in Newport, R.I.

That summer of 1953 I was so full of myself, my accomplishments, the congratulations, the prospects for the future that I must have appeared the pompous ass I realize now how much those status symbols *cost you in dollars, in prayers and patience and how little appreciation I returned to you. My belated and sincere thanks for everything.*

Norm Brown, one of my seminary classmates, had been accepted in the Army Chaplain Corps. Norm, also single, was a couple of years older and wiser in the ways of the world, but we had common roots as farmers' sons from the Midwest. He was a fun-loving guy with a cynical sense of humor, singularly unimpressed with authoritarian figures and institutions. He was to report for duty two months later than me, so we decided that to celebrate our new academic and ecclesiastical achievements he would accompany me on the drive from home to Rhode Island, then as I reported for duty, he would fly home, making a great vacation and our reward for seven years of provincial academia. I picked him up at his father's farm in rural Coal City, Illinois and with ample time to travel we drove up into Canada, down to Niagara Falls, through the Catskills and Connecticut. We stayed at a seaside motel where I got my first view of salt water. It would be our last night out, so we swam in the Ocean, ate at a fancy seafood restaurant and consumed enough sidecars to pickle our minds and bodies. Celebration complete! Men of God indeed! The following morning I drove Norm to the Providence airport, then I continued to Newport, Rhode Island, home of the Navy Chaplain School, the Navy War College and home port to dozens of destroyers and auxiliary ships.

I had two more days before I had to report to the school, so I explored Newport, marveling at the mansions of the rich and famous, sampling numerous varieties of seafood that I had only read about and visiting historical sites in a city that had been founded in 1639. The waterfront was lined with sleek racing yachts from around the world, preparing for the America's Cup race. Several foreign languages could be heard around the boats and in the bars and clubs. The sights and smells were new and exciting like literary legends come alive.

When at last the time had come, I approached the gate guarding the entrance to the Navy base. Dressed in the most casual civilian clothing I showed my orders to the Marine sentry who gave me a temporary pass for my car and directions to the building housing the Chaplain School. I must have appeared as the greenest recruit ever to enter the Navy, dressed in a nylon wash and wear sport shirt and casual trousers. An enlisted clerk took my orders and directed me to the security office to secure an ID card and where I was introduced to the legendary military/government red tape and runaround. The ID card required a photo of me in uniform but I had no uniform. I was therefore directed to the uniform store where I was informed that only people in uniform were admitted. When I tried to explain my predicament I was met with "Regulations are regulations, no exceptions". Likewise when I returned to the security office the answer was the same, "Sorry, no uniform, no ID card." Next, back to the Chaplain School to explain my predicament and seek a solution. It was my good fortune to encounter a newly reported chaplain who had been through the same runaround and who told me of a Max Oberhard who operated a uniform shop in town and who was most accommodating and extended all the credit required. I located Max who outfitted me with a full uniform including the collar devices, gold lace on the sleeves, then custom fitted the uniform to me. Max also showed me how to attach the appropriate insignia of rank and corps, then sent me on my way. "Don't worry about the bill, Chaplain; you can pay me when you draw your uniform allowance." Max was happy to have my business and felt sure that I would be his customer for life.. Dressed in my new uniform I returned to the base, pulled up to the security gate where the Marine sentry rendered a smart salute and waved me through. I thought, I could get used to this.

chapter twelve
CHAPLAIN SCHOOL

I had been unprepared for college, academically and emotionally but somehow I bumbled through with a few supportive faculty and friends. I was truly unprepared for graduate school in theology; motivationally unprepared and academically unprepared, but I struggled through three years and was rewarded with the Master of Divinity degree now handsomely framed. But these struggles through academia were mere bumps in the road compared to the naivety, unsophistication with which I entered "the real world", the world beyond academia, beyond the Midwest and the Presbyterian Church. I was entering a multicultural, multiethnic and multi-theological world of the U.S. Navy Chaplain Corps. I had never been east of Chicago. I had never been west of Rapid City. I had never met a Jew, a Nazarene, a Mormon, a Seventh Day Adventist, or Greek Orthodox person. I had known mostly Midwestern, protestant, white teachers, classmates, neighbors or friends. Within six months of taking my oath of office I would sit in a classroom with fifty clergymen from every denomination I had heard of and some I had not heard of Catholic priests, Christian Science Practitioners, Southern (and several other varieties) Baptists, Lutherans of several sorts, Nazarenes and more. Most were older, some with former military service, as both officer or enlisted. Most had previous experience in some form of civilian ministry. I was probably the youngest and certainly the most "wet behind the ears" of the entire class. Thrust into this theological potpourri, my conservative Midwestern mores were challenged, my parochial perspectives shaken. The Jews embraced the covenants that God gave Abraham, Moses and the prophets. The Catholics claimed that the Pope was the direct successor of Peter, the first Pope and who spoke for God in all matters. The Baptists and other fundamentalists held that only through embracing the Plan of Salvation with its doctrines of original sin, substitution atonement, and experience rebirth would one attain salvation. My own beliefs first laid down at home and church, later altered by various professors and authors in seminary were in a state of flux. We fledging chaplains, fine gentlemen with mutually exclusive beliefs would go off to lunch together and share a double room in the barracks. In their future ministries aboard ship where each was the only clergy on board, each would facilitate layman-led worship of numerous denominations other than his own. Thus we were introduced to the Chaplain Corps motto, "Cooperation Without Compromise".

The curriculum was relatively easy. Basic orientation to the Navy, ranks and rates, types of ships and shore stations, Uniform Code of Military Justice, Navy rules and regulations, pass a swimming test, wear a gas mask, use firefighting equipment, first aid and, yes, march in formation, drilled by a Marine Corps Sargent. We embarked on a destroyer for a one-day "orientation cruise" and where I became seriously seasick. What am I getting myself into, I thought.

We were free on weekends to explore and enjoy the sights, attractions and activities of Newport, the town founded in 1626, centuries before white men had set foot in Windom, Minnesota.

Little did I know on those carefree days that six months after taking the oath I would see both the Atlantic and Pacific oceans, would travel by auto from coast to coast, cross the Pacific in a Navy ship and ride a taxi down the streets of Yokohama.

※ ※ ※ ※

chapter thirteen
FIRST DUTY STATION

Remember when I came home on my first leave in the fall of 1953? I strutted my stuff with a Master of Divinity degree, Ordination by the laying on of hands, commission in the U. S. Navy and wearing the gold trimmed uniform, on my way to a life of fabled adventure and excitement. What a pompous clown! I still had so much to learn, such need to mature.

Completion of Chaplain School, October 22, 1953 was marked by a graduation ceremony and delivery of orders to 42 freshly minted Navy clergy, their gold insignia yet untarnished by ocean spray. My orders arrived by teletype in very cryptic format.

"From: The Bureau of Naval Personnel

To: LTJG Donald A. Weir, CHC, USNR 828257

Subject: Change of Duty.

1. On or about October 1, 1953, and when directed by your commanding officer, proceed and report to the Commanding Officer of North Pacific Sea Transportation Command, Seattle, Washington for further assignment to duty at sea.
2. Provided no excess leave is involved, you are further authorized thirty days delay in reporting, such delay to count as leave.
3. Travel by privately owned vehicle is authorized. The following entries consisted of accounting data and Bureau of Personnel authorizing directives.

When the orders had been distributed to all of us, we were assembled in the classroom for a lesson in reading Navy gobbledygook. For example, when official orders employed the term "proceed" it meant that we have four days to pack our gear, say our goodbyes and complete any personal or business affairs, not to count as leave. When travelling by "POV", privately owned vehicle' is authorized, I must travel a given number of miles daily, not to count as leave. Likewise, "report to the commanding officer" did not mean finding the admiral, knocking on his door to say, "Here I am, sir", but report to the personnel office where a petty officer would log me officially aboard with an endorsement of my orders and direct me to the appropriate officer who would be my immediate superior and supervisor.

I wasted no time in loading my uniforms, civvies and few personal possessions into the Chevy and headed west. We were required to travel a minimum of 250 miles each day, but I made about 500 miles daily thereby accruing additional days not to count against my 30 days of annual leave. I routed myself through

Windom to drive around town in my uniform in my shiny new Chevrolet! How vain! How pretentious, how supercilious! After a brief visit with my parents and other family, especially the crown prince, now a mail carrier and the Pink Princess, now doing clerical work at the University, I continued west.

It was, and still is, a long, bleak ride across South Dakota. I had been to the Black Hills but no farther west. I had been advised not to drive the northern route across the mountains as there were heavy snow advisories with some places impassable, so I headed southwest towards Denver. When the Rocky Mountains first appeared on the horizon, they literally took my breath away. There is no way I could have anticipated their magnificence. I still had hours of driving before reaching the foothills, and finally Denver with its elevation of five thousand feet and for which it has earned its nickname "The Mile High City".

From Denver I took U.S. Highway 40 west and noticed the elevation continued to climb. Roadside signs began to warn of heavy snow ahead, and not to proceed without tire chains. Well, I had no chains, and I had driven in plenty of snow in Minnesota. My tires were new so I pressed on, noticing an occasional car that had slid off the road. More signs indicated that we were now above 10,000 feet elevation, my car labored in the thin air and the tires let the car "fishtail" a couple of times. Suddenly the back wheels of the car slid off the right shoulder, overlooking a very steep slope. Luckily the front wheels clung to the gravel edge of the road. I opened the door gently and looked down, shuddered at my near demise. Had I travelled a foot farther it would have been sudden death. It was my good fortune that a huge snowplow came along, towed the car back onto the highway and followed me the remaining two miles to the summit. I was amazed to discover that the roads on the western slope were dry and clear of snow, so the remainder of the trip was uneventful. Descending from the continental divide I marveled at the beauty of the mountains and forests. When I reached Seattle, I found the waterfront where Navy ships were moored. I followed the signs to a Marine sentry who asked to see my I.D. card, then with a legendary "buggy whip" salute, waved me in.

My superior officer turned out to be a four stripe (rank of captain) chaplain with a second story office overlooking Eliot Bay where numerous Navy ships and other watercraft could be seen.. He gave me a short briefing on my duties, then assigned me to USNS HUGH J. GAFFEY, a large personnel transport carrying military personnel and their dependents between our west coast and the Far East. Navy ships are all designated USS, for United States Ship, and the crews are all navy officers and enlisted. Gaffey, a personnel carrier, was designated USNS for U.S. Naval Ship, operated by Merchant Marine crew, but carried a small Navy contingent to process passengers and provide certain services. I was to provide ministry to all persons aboard, crew and passengers of all, or no, faiths. Gaffey was scheduled to sail in four days for Yokohama Japan carrying mostly Army troops bound for Korea and some for other service in the Far East. There were also the families under orders to stations where there were accommodations for family living.

Although a truce had been signed ending hostilities in Korea we still had thousands of troops stationed there. There were also military personnel whose families accompanied them to Japan, Okinawa, Guam, Taiwan, and Hawaii. Aboard Gaffey I was assigned a comfortable stateroom on the main deck with a private head (bathroom), a porthole providing a view, a bunk, closet and desk. I also had a private office, small but adequate with shelves for books and two guest chairs. I was excited over the prospects of visiting the exotic destinations on our schedule. That euphoria would soon vanish when we steamed into the open Pacific and the ship began a steady roll. In a matter of hours I was seasick, violent, retching seasick, thinking that I had chosen wrongly, that I was being punished for pretending to be something I was not. With my head in the toilet retching my guts out I was definitely not the Knight-in-Blue of my adolescent dreams.

In about forty-eight hours I had found my sea legs, presented myself at the dinner table designated for the Navy officers of the Military Department. Weak, hungry and the target of many friendly jibes and remarks about my recent malaise, I was introduced to the others at the table; the Officer in Charge, his assistant, two medical officers, two nurses, and two supply officers., forming an amiable and cohesive group.

There were only general written directives or instructions for my position, so I spent most of the crossing getting to know the ship and its crew, designing some elements of a program for whatever spiritual needs I found, conducting Sunday worship and a daily devotion for the passengers.

When we steamed into Tokyo Bay at dawn to dock at the port of Yokohama I looked out at a world I had only seen in war movies; but now missing was the huge Japanese fleet that had first bombed Pearl Harbor and with whom we had engaged in awesome sea battles at memorable islands across the Pacific. Also missing was the site where history was made, the battleship USS MISSOURI, where the Emperor of Japan and General MacArthur formally signed the surrender documents ending World War II. Now the bay was dotted with small fishing boats and commercial vessels moored at the piers. A dense industrial haze (smog) enveloped the city, and the noise of commerce was everywhere.

One of the ship's surgeons took me ashore to acquaint me with the city and to keep me from getting lost and out of trouble. He hailed a cab, a tiny vehicle built to accommodate the much smaller Japanese passengers, shouted something in Japanese and we were off. We raced down the narrow streets on the wrong (left) side, the horn blasting people and vehicles out of the way. My knuckles turned white as I gripped the door handle, ready to bail out. Doc joked that the cabbie was a former Kamikaze pilot who had survived the war. The cab screeched to a halt and the driver shouted what sounded like "Motomachi", and we stepped out unharmed but shaken.

Doc explained that Motomachi was the name of the street

that looked more like an alley, lined with shops, most open to the street, and that sold all matters of objects Japanese. I remember lots of "ivory" chop sticks, brass book ends, many examples of decorated china plates and cups, and "silk" kimonos. The shopkeepers were mostly diminutive women, bowing and greeting us in broken English. The images of these people during the war as barbaric infidels determined to conquer and destroy America portrayed by cartoonists in the media appeared in my mind. These were the people whose relatives were incinerated at Hiroshima and Nagasaki. These were the people whose sons and husbands had attacked Pearl Harbor, sank our ships and slain our troops on a score of islands across the Pacific. These appeared to be real, warm human beings.

On a train to Tokyo we passed miles of rubble, once emblems of a thriving industrial economy and now the charred remains of General Doolittle's raid. As we travelled around the country we saw Buddhist and Shinto shrines and temples everywhere reminding me that here were races and religions that predated our religions, predated Europeans "discovering" and settling the United States. I wondered, are these the pagan hoards for which we prayed and to which we sent missionaries to convert them to Christianity? Are these polite and gentle people condemned to hell because they have not walked down the "sawdust trail" at a revival meeting".

In Gaffey, and subsequently Patrick, I made a round trip from Seattle to Yokohama every month and sometimes to the ports of Inchon, Korea, Taiwan, Formosa, Okinawa and Guam. In each instance we disembarked troops, dependents and cargo, then embarking those bound for home in the USA. On two occasions the ship returned to San Francisco rather than Seattle providing my first opportunity to explore some of the wonders of that great city by the Golden Gate.

Throughout the voyages I conducted "daily devotions" and Sunday worship, both were sparsely attended. I had kept the manuscripts of those sermons I had shamelessly "borrowed" from books and journals during seminary years and recycled them with few updates and when ashore searched religious bookstores for additional homiletical fodder for my mill. My duties gave me ample time for reading and I continued to read the Bible, biblical commentaries and theological journals. But always, I was searching for something I could with conscience preach, teach and adapt to the expectations of the position, some words of hope and consolation for the few who attended. I continued to use the Psalms and the Sermon on the Mount as the basis for my homilies, finding universal themes of hope, comfort and a spiritual life.

The ship's crew generally accepted me, even those who had no time for church or religion of any kind, but respected my office and treated me with some deference. The Captain had humorously made me "Officer in Charge of the Weather". When the weather at sea turned bad he would summon me to the bridge and demand that I bring calmer seas. I would reply, "Captain, I'm in Sales, not Management ."

As an early riser I often went to the bridge to observe sunrise, usually a spectacular sight at sea. Herb, the Third Mate and Navigator stood the morning watch. Young and single, we had become good friends. He usually ordered up fresh coffee and pastry from the ship's bakery and he was "shooting the stars", taking the morning position with the sextant. We chatted about mutual interests and experiences. While in Seattle he took me fishing on Puget Sound in his boat. One incident to illustrate that life on the bridge was not always chatty.

We were moored in the port of Taipei, Taiwan, mostly discharging cargo. For political reasons we were not permitted to go ashore so crew, passengers including dependent wives and children, even kennels on the open deck astern, sweltered in the tropical heat. One of the civilian crewmen had slipped ashore, got himself wildly drunk, was arrested and returned to the ship under guard. Captain Healy, a really old time Master of the Vessel, had him confined to the ship's brig, basically a cage in the bow of the ship, located directly under the steel deck with no air conditioning or ventilation. . The temperature outside was well over 100 so the sun beating down on that steel deck created a veritable oven. The prisoner sent for me and I visited him briefly, repulsed by the heat and the stench of the place. I felt that it was really inhuman treatment and hurried to the bridge to intercede with the Captain for the poor wretch below. I was not well received. As I can best recall he said , The man deserved no better and I will deal with him when we were underway again. I responded, "Even the dogs had fresh air to breathe". He bristled, got red in the face and ordered me off the bridge and to mind my own business. I obeyed. It was several days at sea before I ventured up to join Herb for our morning repast. The captain appeared unexpectedly early and said, "Where have you been hiding, Padre? I haven't seen you in some time". "The last time I was up here it was uncomfortably warm", I replied. "Well, you made me mad, saying I treated my crew worse than the dogs." I replied, "Well.....and we both let it drop at that.

Also in Seattle, three of the young Navy officers decided to take me out on the town and celebrate my 25th birthday. We were all suffering from the "cabin fever" of weeks at sea and were ready to blow off a little steam. We had dinner followed by visiting a few night spots around town. Finally at Trader Vic's bar in the Benjamin Franklin hotel one of our party, emboldened by too many "Fog Cutters", took a fancy to the little copper lanterns on each table. He blew out the candle and stuffed a lantern under his topcoat and headed for the exit. There he was apprehended by security and shown the door and the remaining three of us were stuck with his bar bill. Somehow we all found our way back to the ship, and the next day suffered greatly for our revelry.

The most memorable experience of two years in troop ships began in December 1954. Moored in Seattle with a welcome lull between trips, the Navy had approved my plans to spend Christmas with my family in Minnesota. The travel authorization papers were in hand and the flight reservations were made when I was abruptly summoned to my supervisory chaplain's office and notified that my Christmas leave was cancelled and in four days I would be sailing in USNS MARINE SERPENT on an extended mission. The SERPENT, an aged troop ship irreverently dubbed SEA SNAKE and it had seen better days. Our destination was Viet Nam, a country known until recently as French Indo China. The Geneva Convention of 1954 had divided the country at the 17th parallel, thereby creating North Viet Nam (communist) and South Viet Nam (democratic). The French troops who had for years occupied the country were leaving. According to the treaty, Vietnamese citizens were given the opportunity to move from one side of the line or the other. Tens of thousands of Vietnamese in the north chose to move south to live under the democratic regime.

The United States government had launched "Operation Passage to Freedom", a program that provided transportation and other support to these refugees. Marine Serpent was one of several ships sent to embark people at Haiphong, port city of Hanoi in the North, and carry them to Saigon, then the capital of the newly formed government of South Viet Nam.

Large numbers of those choosing to go south were Tonkinese, Roman Catholics, organized and encouraged by their bishops to flee the persecutions expected from the communist government. Others included the Montgnards, an ethnic group of tribes from the northern highlands, some Buddhists, and some other native religions. "Serpent" made numerous round trips carrying these groups of ethnic, racial and religious mix. They came aboard our ship by the thousands, carrying all of their possessions possible. Many of the tribal people had never seen plumbing so used any available space to perform their bathroom functions. The ship was prepared to feed these passengers, but many chose to cook their rice over open flames throughout the living spaces, creating a stench and a great risk of burning the ship's equipment. Gone was the spit and polish for which the Navy was known.

I tried to be of assistance wherever possible. As a Presbyterian clergyman amid 5000 refugees of Buddhist, Catholic and tribal religions, my traditional rites and services that included "Amazing Grace" and "The Old Rugged Cross" were not on the top ten of the Buddhist's Hit Parade. I did not see these people as depraved and condemned to hell and to be converted to western religions and cultures, but as fellow humans placed here by time and fate and doing their utmost to survive and make a life for themselves and their families. I distributed soap, candy bars and other personal items to many who had to leave such items behind. Now, for the first time in weeks they were able to wash themselves and their babies. "Jesus said, "Whoever gives even a cup of cold water to one of these little ones in the name of a disciple...truly I tell you none of these will lose their reward." I felt that these simple acts of mercy were more "Jesus-like" than all the Western dogma, Catholic or Protestant. Many millions of Asians had practiced their rites centuries before Christianity was born. These poor transient and homeless people that I had served today are the same people that fundamentalist sects condemned to hell because they had not "accepted Jesus as their Lord and Savior"? Televangelists such as Billy Graham would rant that "all people are sinners and condemned to hell unless they are born again" and then his biographers boasted of the thousands to whom Graham had "brought to Christ". I questioned, are these displaced humans who are only seeking peace and a home, targets for missionaries of several denominations to "convert", to abandon their traditions, beliefs and faith? What did my culture, my traditions, my theological training ask of me in this foreign milieu?

All of my traditions and training were being challenged. The doctrine of salvation proclaimed by learned seminary professors seemed less relevant than handing a bar of soap so these nomadic peasants. may bathe their babies. "Whoever gives even a 'a bar of soap, a piece of chocolate, a bag of rice" to one of these little ones in the name of a disciple...truly I tell you, none of these will lose their reward." Matthew 10:42. Here was the practical application of the second great commandment: "Love your neighbor as yourself ". My mind kept returning to Absalom Sydenstricker, Pearl Buck's father, a fundamentalist Presbyterian minister who spent 10 years as a missionary to China. The Chinese villagers were not impressed with his fire and brimstone preaching. The Reverend Sydenstricker estimated that in ten years he had made ten converts.

While disembarking our passengers into trucks destined for resettlement camps I went ashore in Saigon where I discovered a great contrast of cultures. There were a few remaining French colonials who could be seen around the luxurious Majestic Hotel while the poor, the homeless urchins begged for coins or pimped for prostitutes. One afternoon I sat on the patio of the Majestic, sipping a cool drink and contemplating this mysterious world and my place in it.

My brain was overloaded with the experiences of the past eighteen months. For the first time in my life I had departed the Midwest with its conservative, parochial agricultural culture. I had driven to the east coast, experienced the sights, sounds, tastes and power of the Atlantic Ocean. I had lived in close quarters and studied with clergymen of religious sects and domination coming from ghettos, races and cultures of inner city to rural rustic. I had been immersed in the history and traditions of the U. S. Navy.

Then I had traveled the breadth of the continent seeing for the first time mountains, canyons, bridges, dams and rivers that had previously been marks on a map or pictures in a magazine. A dozen crossings of the Pacific had introduced me to Asia with its multiple races, its cultures, and languages. And now, here in a city of foreign tongue, culture, climate and war, a city in which fate has dropped me. Aboard the troop ships bound both to and from the war in Korea I met G.I.s from every corner of every state in the union, each from his own culture, each with or without his religion and values.

of seeming irrelevance of much that I had been taught, all the doctrines and sacraments of Christianity.

At sea I had time and inclination to review the relevance between the teachings of church and seminary and the life and teachings of Jesus. The first three centuries A.D. saw the church evolve from family groups gathering in homes, there to be taught by Jesus or his disciples to a complex organization of bishops in cities throughout the Roman Empire. The Emperor Constantine noting the divisive teachings of the bishoprics called them all together demanding that they speak with one voice. The result was the Nicene Creed to which all Romans were required to believe, sometimes enforced by torture or death. The bishop of Rome was made Pope, and the pope's powers grew enforcing the allegiance to the church and the emperor. "Enforcing" included torture, imprisonment, execution and war. I never did understand the concept of cardinals came into being, only that they were political appointees with power to enforce the Pope's edicts and demands.

Attempts to reform the church over centuries broke into hundreds of new denominations such as Lutheran, Presbyterian, Reformed, Baptist and many, many others, and in my opinion, most of these grew further away from the teachings and practices of Jesus. They structured denominations consisting of presidents, district superintendents, vicars. Elders, deacons and ministers. Many of these sects or denominations ignored or disbelieved the discoveries of the sciences, astronomy, physics and medicine.

There were signs of the yet-to-be-named New Age. I thought of the battle-hardened troops we had returned from Korea, who had largely ignored the religious services on the ship. Many had been introduced to marijuana and other drugs. Most had killed and seen their buddies killed or maimed and now responded with cynicism or detachment. Now I was confronted by the millions of foreign natives who had their own religions, rites and traditions. The religion and culture in which I was reared and educated seemed irrelevant to life as I was now experiencing it.

So when the Presbytery of Mankato suggested I return and serve as pastor to a village church much like the one of my childhood, the church from which I had wandered so far, I felt pressured to make a hard choice. Should I return to serve a church much like the church of my youth, farmers and villagers whose beliefs and expectations had not changed in a century; beliefs that I could no longer embrace but would be happily embraced by rural folks in the Corn Belt. Should I continue in the Navy, acting out the role of the office and wrestling with my doubts and changing beliefs? Should I "chuck it all" and seek a new vocation where there was no expectations of my personal faith or lack thereof? Was this the inner struggle between the "good son and the bad son"? Is there work to be done in a changing world, a changing church that has not yet been revealed? I was living between the middle ages and the emerging New Age.

The return trip to Seattle included a weeklong stay in Japan for the ship to be thoroughly cleaned and sanitized. The leisurely crossing of the pacific gave me time to read and think of my future. One day I came upon William E. Barrett's novel, "The Left Hand of God" which gave me a new idea. The plot ran thus: Jim Carmody American pilot had been shot down over a remote area of China, had survived and was pressed into involuntary service of a distant war lord. He eventually escaped and traveled at night through remote and isolated areas. He came upon the body of a priest who had been killed by outlaws, switched clothing with the corpse and proceeded to flee in clerical garb and came to a Catholic mission where he was welcomed as the long awaited, now slain, pastor of the mission. With the help of an unsuspecting altar boy he proceeded to perform the priestly functions, celebrating mass, hearing confessions and baptizing babies and converts. The Chinese people loved him in spite of his discomfort in the role. Falling in love with the nurse complicated the situation. When by mail he conveyed the truth of his identity to the Bishop in a distant city, a relief priest was dispatched at once to relieve him. The bishop arrived with the new, bone fide priest and swore Carmody to secrecy, remarking at the replacement service, "God does not always use the conventional means to carry on His work." Perhaps what I believe is less important than what I do. Does distributing food to thousands trump ten years of peaching for one soul? What do these musings speak to the next years of my ministry?

By the time we docked in Seattle I still had more questions than answers. Weary of the uncertainty and the inner arguing, I yielded to the voice of my childhood, pleading "be a good boy, Donnie, the Big People know best", and decided to return to civilian life, to accept the counsel of Presbytery to accept one of the "vacant pulpits", stuff my doubts and play the role that was expected of me. Was I a present day Jim Carmody, going through the motions, concealing my true identity and trusting that God's work does not depend on my beliefs, or lack thereof.

The drive back to Minnesota was a leisurely and pleasant one, three days of solitude to further contemplate my decision, my future, and my life. Was I compromising my deepest beliefs? What did I really believe and what was my purpose in life? I recalled an anonymous quote: "Faith is believing what you know isn't true". Is it too late to start my life over at age 26?

It was midday when I pulled into my parents' retirement farm, thirty or so acres on the banks of the Des Moines River and three miles out of Windom. They leased the tillable land to neighboring farmers while they both held jobs in town. I parked my sporty new Chevy near the garage. I stepped out into a beautiful summer day and felt a wave of nostalgia envelop me. I lay down under a huge cottonwood tree, feeling the rough warmth of native soil. I closed my eyes and fell asleep to the lullaby of the summer breeze ruffling the Cottonwood leaves above. I awoke and picked up the script that Presbytery handed me, but I would recall that moment years later as I read Mary Oliver's poem, "I thought the earth remembered me, she took me back so tenderly, arranging her dark skirts, her pocket full of lichens and seeds. I slept as never before......"

chapter fourteen
RETURNING, RETREATING

It was good to be home again, to be with family, to walk the soil, attend the animals and connect with my roots. You welcomed me so warmly, treated me as a celebrity with my blue uniform, gold stripes and service ribbons. I was displayed at your church and at family gatherings and your pride showed. But behind the blue and gold, buried behind a smiling facade was a different person than the one who left your home nine years previously. I had been exposed to every branch of Christianity as well as Judaism, Buddhism, Shintoism, and native religions whose names

I do not know. They were no longer pagans described in a book, but people, individuals who had families, children, and parents, and who struggled to survive, to live in peace. I no longer believed that Protestant Christianity had exclusive knowledge of truth. I could no longer recite the creeds. I partook of the sacrament only to avoid conflicts and disappointments. I could not break your hearts seeing me labeled "heretic".

All of this was carried on at a subconscious level. I stuffed it in the closet of the unconscious, slammed the door and turned the key. I picked up the script, assumed the role handed to me by The Big People. The ultimate pretense was accepting the call to a village church, and as I did I had a new appreciation of the Reverend Arthur Dimmesdale portrayed in Hawthorne's "The Scarlet Letter". Dimmesdale had fathered the child of Hester Prynne and both of them kept it a secret for years while he continued to serve as vicar. I had sired no illegitimate children but had my own secrets, hidden behind my own facade. I hid behind the Bishop's logic, ""God does not always use the conventional means to carry on His work."

Mom and Dad, I have carried this in my secret heart for years. It is only, in this place that I am able to articulate the struggle of my soul these many years.

chapter fifteen
FIRST PRESBYTERIAN
CHURCH OF BEAVER CREEK

The Navy released me from active duty in Seattle in June 1955. I was 26 years old, single and spiritually floundering. I thought that if I returned to my roots, to the culture of my youth, I could find peace of mind and a renewal of my vocation. I was re-entering the culture from which I had fled after high school, the same doctrines that I had secretly ignored and the same rural mores that I had found so restrictive. At age 26 it was also time to think seriously about marriage and family, and the prospects at sea were not promising.

I was installed as the minister of The First Presbyterian Church of Beaver Creek, Minnesota, a village in southwestern Minnesota located about sixty miles from Windom, my home town and about twenty-five miles the state lines of both Iowa and South Dakota. Had I come full circle? The village consisted of one general store, one café, one gas station, one post office, one liquor store, one bank, two churches and a public school teaching all twelve grades. The good people of Beaver Creek (many locals pronounced it Crick) welcomed me even though they had just completed building a new manse, (minister's house) hoping to attract a young married couple to their church. The mothers of a couple of eligible young ladies were not so disappointed.

The people's expectations of me were easily fulfilled; nearly identical to the congregation in which I was reared: to preach every Sunday, to mentor the youth group, call on the sick and infirm, administer the sacraments of baptism and the Lord's Supper, moderate meetings of the session and, of course, represent the church at meetings of Mankato Presbytery. My inventory of sermons was recycled with some rural applications.

> *"I always voted at my part's beck and call*
> *and never thought of thinking for myself at all."*
> Sir Joseph Porter
> HMS Pinafore

Occasionally my parents drove down from Windom to hear their preacher son whose education had cost them dearly. Their pride in me shone in their faces. My lifestyle was simple. I subsisted on simple home cooking in the sparsely furnished in the three bedroom manse with an occasional meal at the local café or a sumptuous meal in the home of one of the flock, a fine old Midwestern tradition.

I applied myself diligently to these duties, closing my mind to the questions and uncertainties that had plagued these many years. Beaver Creek was surrounded by miles farms located on rich, fertile soil. Church membership consisted mostly of farm families and retired farmers. To these good people I related easily, to their concerns, the weather, for their livelihood depended on adequate rainfall and absence of hail, frost, animal disease and stable market prices for their crops and livestock.

My social life consisted mainly of three other young bachelors forming a foursome for bridge at the manse. The high school band and chorus conductor, the high school athletic coach, and a bank teller joined me weekly for a rubber of bridge and small talk. Twice I dated young ladies of the church whose parents thought the young preacher would make a "good catch" for a farmer's daughter and the flock applauded silently. Remembering the admonition in Genesis One, "It is not good for man to be alone:" I took each to dinner and a movie in neighboring towns. They were attractive, pleasant company but there was "no magic" and the relationships were short lived. The girls and their families were of the same cultural fabric for which I had fled Windom. In fact, I was growing weary of the whole routine. I found little opportunity to grow mentally and spiritually. Had the inner voice been silenced? Had I sold out to the Big People? I slammed the door on those questions and took up my duties with bravado if not commitment. I applied myself diligently and continued stuffing these questions and uncertainties into the now crowded unconscious. In the Spring of 1957, I was invited to join a group of ministers of several denominations from surrounding towns who met weekly during Lent to study and discuss biblical texts recommended by the churches for this season, and from which we would be preaching the following Sunday. It was in these informal sessions that some of us found the courage to speak of our doubts, to question some of the tenants, creeds and teachings of our churches. One of our number spoke of his loss of his "call", that he no longer felt called to his vocation, that he may have made a mistake. He was in his forties and serving a large congregation with a generous budget and a comfortable salary. He also had a wife who loved expensive things, furnishings, clothing and lifestyle and two children nearing college age who would be needing tuition, board, room, books and incidentals, so he felt "trapped" in his present position, unable or unwilling to accept an entry position in a new career. He slogged through the weekly routine for which he was being paid. I wondered how many other clergy harbored secret doubts behind the façade of piety and the expectations of the people who supported them. The wall behind which I kept my doubts about both the theology and church government of the church was continuing to fracture. My serious differences with the creeds and catechisms that were part of education and culture were straining for expression. and I had been experiencing a growing empty spot in my life and in my heart. In my prayers I cried out for a mate. For years I had pushed it out of my consciousness; "stuffed it" like other needs and longings, but it would no longer be denied.

During Advent, 1956, I was 28 years old, and Christmas was rapidly approaching. Holiday lights and Christmas trees glowed in homes, in stores and in public places. Christmas carols and other holiday music played in stores, on radios everywhere. I was preaching from the advent texts, coordinating decorating of the church, rehearsals of choral music, children's' pageants. The pace of life in the village turned brisk, matching the signs of early winter, snow, ice skates and snow shovels. The church and the community were anticipating Christmas Eve marked by the annual children's programs, pageants, carols and sacraments. The Christmas Eve service at First Presbyterian consisted of the children's pageant with wise men and shepherds appropriately attired in costumes fashioned from feed sacks and bed sheets. Mary and her infant, Jesus, amid assorted animals and fresh straw formed the obligatory centerpiece. The finale was the lighting of the candles and singing "Silent Night", before the benediction.

As families moved out of the church and towards heir cars calling out "Merry Christmas" to each other, I walked the twenty paces next door to the manse. It was a crisp, sub-zero Minnesota winter evening. The stars seemed to shine with extra brilliance, as did the Star on that first Christmas so long ago.

When I entered the house I was startled by the silence, the emptiness that reflected the emptiness of my life. No mate in my arms! No voices of children! No music, not even a pet! Pictures of Christmases past in my childhood arose in my mind: *"Hurry with the chores don't be late for church , we must be on time for the Christmas program." Afterwards, home to turn the crank on the ice cream freezer. The aroma of homemade apple pie floated from the kitchen.... . opening the long awaited gifts.....hand tools, erector set, ice skates and not uncommonly new shoes or overalls...*

suitable for farm boys and practical for parents trying at once to be generous and thrifty in the depths of the depression.

But that was then and this was now.

I continued down the short hallway and looked in at the empty double bed, and that's where I "lost it". The inner wall that had held my emotions at bay, my hopes, my dreams, my disappointments, my utter loneliness and despair, crumbled. Fully clothed, I sprawled face down on the bed and wept. I sobbed, cried out to God. In my loneliness, my emptiness and despair. I questioned everything about my life. Had I misread my "call" to ministry? Should I have stayed on the farm and married a farmer's daughter? Should I have persisted in enlisting in the Army when the urge was fresh? Am I sentenced to tis life of pretension and isolation? I intoned the cry of Jesus from the cross, "My God, my God, why have you forsaken me." I sobbed myself to exhaustion and fell at last into restless sleep.

I awoke spent, hungry, feeling abandoned and utterly alone. I showered, dressed warmly, and walked to the local café for coffee only to find a sign on the door, "CLOSED FOR THE HOLIDAY'. I turned and plodded home. Lighted Christmas trees shone through the windows of "my people". The shrieks of children opening gifts punctuated my loneliness as I continued on home, heated day-old coffee, and munched on an ageing donut. I felt even more alone and wallowed in self-pity. The words of last night's sacrament came to mind, "Tthis is my body broken for you, this is my blood shed for you, do this in remembrance of me.." "In remembrance of me", remembrance of the One who was abandoned by his disciples when he was tortured and slain, the One who walked alone without spouse, family or friend, "despised and rejected by men", the One who went to the cross in the company of thieves. Is this to be my life also?

In the weeks to come I moved trancelike through my duties with bravado if not inner commitment. I was hardly a model of leadership for those who wrote the monthly check. "Let the Big

People rule, Goofus. Who do you think you are? Somebody special?"

Relief came suddenly and unexpectedly that week. I tore open a familiar looking envelope and read the official letterhead:

From: The Chief of Naval Personnel

To: Lieutenant Donald A. Weir, CHC, USNR

Subject: Promotion and recall to active duty.

1. You have been selected for promotion to the rank of lieutenant effective July 1, 1957.
2. On or about August 1, 1957 proceed and report to Commander Cruiser-Destroyer Force Atlantic Fleet, Newport R.I. for further assignment to sea duty.

This was followed by the usual accounting data and travel instructions.

I must go down to the sea again,
to the lonely sea and the tide,
and all I ask is a tall ship
and a star to steer her by.

John Masefield

chapter sixteen
BACK TO THE SEA

You must have had questions about my decision to return to the Navy, but you kept your peace and wished me well. I did not understand it myself; however, I felt truly called to make this move, little knowing what great changes lay ahead, changes in my understanding of the gospel, changes in the shape of my ministry. Like Mary who could not understand the words of her son, kept her peace and "treasured all these things in her heart".

> *Some went down to the sea in ships,*
> *doing business on the mighty waters;*
> *they saw the deeds of the Lord,*
> *his wondrous works in the deep.*
>
> Psalm 107:23

I placed my meager household furniture in storage, packed my uniforms and personal gear, pointed the Chevy toward Newport and settled in for a comfortable three-day drive. I had phoned two seminary classmates who lived more or less on the way, arranging a stopover visit with them. I found them in much the same situation as I was leaving, serving small churches but settled into comfortable parish routines, married with children and a dog. I sensed no evidence of the angst that plagued my soul. My visits with these guys confirmed my decision return to the Navy.

> *I must go down to the seas again, for the call of the running tide*
> *Is a wild call and a clear call that may not go denied;*
> *And all I ask is a windy day with the white clouds flying,*
> *And the flung spray and the blown*
> *spume, and the sea-gulls crying.*

It was good to be back in Newport, breathing the salt air, hearing the fog horns in the night, and watching the maritime traffic during the day. Two more travel days remained on my orders which I used to have Max re-stripe my uniforms with the new rank, to tour the city's sights and swim in the ocean. A dozen or so Navy ships were tied up at piers or moored to buoys in Narragansett Bay. My decision was confirmed. It felt right to be here. On a fine autumn morning I donned a freshly pressed uniform, pulled up to a security post manned by a Marine corporal who rendered a signature "buggy whip" salute and motioned me past a sign that read:

COMMANDER DESTROYER SQUADRONS ATLANTIC NEWPORT, RHODE ISLAND

I soon learned to translate the sign in the new Navy shorthand: COMDESLANT

I followed directional signs to the headquarters buildings finding my way to the office of the Captain McQuaid, Staff Chaplain, a crusty old Catholic Priest wearing the four stripes of his rank and a chest full of ribbons that spoke of many years of service. He greeted me with, "I hope your sea bags are packed, sailor, you are going to sea on Monday". Then he handed me an endorsement to my orders:

From: Commander Destroyer Force Atlantic

To: LT Donald A. Weir, CHC, USNR

Subject: Orders to duty.

1. *You will report immediately to Commander Destroyer Squadron Twelve for duty on his staff. No leave, travel or delay is authorized.*

/s/ Raymond Sartorius, by direction.

"You will be working for Commodore Grimshaw Moore, Fr. McQuaid said as we chatted informally for a few minutes. "Commodore Moore is one of the most respected officers in the fleet, academy graduate and veteran on many a battle in the Pacific." Just then a young officer wearing a uniform identical to mine entered the room. "This is Charlie Clark. You will be relieving him in Squadron Twelve and I asked him to introduce you to the commodore and show you around a bit.

Dismissed by Fr. McQuaid we walked down Pier One where Bill motioned to eight nearly identical ships moored two abreast and each sporting the identical logo on the forward stack: a single di thrown so only the one spot and the two spot were showing, "ace and deuce, known throughout the fleet as the Acey/Duecy squadron". With an inclusive wave of his arm Charlie declared, "Here's your parish, Padre."

We paused so I could begin to take it all in, as he continued to recite a string of facts....the history of the squadron, the equipment on each ship, and a summary of the work he had performed during the several cruises in the two years just past. In the coming months I would learn for myself the esprit de corps of destroyer men, these "tin can sailors". The crews of larger ships, the aircraft carriers, battleships and cruisers referred to destroyers as "Tin Cans" or "Small Boys, but the men who served aboard "cans" were fiercely proud of their vessels. Many had served aboard their ships since commissioning day and had seen combat in the Pacific, wreaking havoc on the Japanese fleet with their five inch guns and torpedoes, depth charging their submarines and shooting their aircraft into the sea in battles like Leyte Gulf and Midway. The original crewmembers of Navy ships were known as "plank owners", a term carried over from the days of "wooden ships and iron men". These eight crews were now proud to be a part of the Acey-Deucy squadron.

As we proceeded down the pier Bill called out the hull number and name of each ship.

USS COMPTON DD705
USS GAINARD DD 706
USS DICKSON DD708
USS PURVIS DD 709
USS HYMAN DD 732
USS PURDY DD734
USS BEATY DD 756
USS BRISTOL DD 857

All eight were of the twenty-four hundred ton Alan M. Sumner class; all were built in 1944 and sent immediately into battle. Each ship was fitted with four 5 inch 58 caliber guns forward and two aft. They were also equipped with 20 caliber anti-aircraft guns, torpedoes, depth charges and other weapons. GAINARD was the flagship of the squadron, carrying the commodore and his staff. I noted that on each ship the crews, wearing dungarees and the signature "Dixie Cup" hats, were busy chipping paint, repainting, and loading supplies. The entire area buzzed with activity. Fresh water lines and electrical cable stretched from the pier to the ships allowing the ships to shut down engines and equipment for repairs and maintenance. Bill took me aboard GAINARD to meet the Commodore, the overall commander of the eight ship squadron, a Navy Captain, who bore the title "Commodore" in this position, so as not to be confused with "Captain", the honorary title of any officer who commands a ship, regardless of his Navy rank. Most of the captains of the destroyers bore the Navy rank of commander. I was assigned to the commodore's staff and had responsibility for the religious program in each of the ships. Bill gave me a quick resume of the commodore: Naval Academy class of 1932 where he was called by his middle name, Girmshaw, and still is by his peers. As Captain of USS Kidd he had been awarded the Silver Star and Purple heart for gallantry in combat in action against the Japanese navy." Bill noted, "Easy to work for, supportive, demanding but not micromanager."

We climbed the ladders to the Commodore's quarters directly aft of the bridge where I met the legendary Captain Harry Grimshaw Moore. Sparkling blue eyes looked out of his ruddy complexion, weathered by years at sea, and his warm smile that confirmed his "Welcome aboard, Padre". I was soon to learn that he was a highly respected destroyerman and DESRON TWELVE, the Acey-Deucy squadron was proud to have him in command. "We are leaving next week for training with NATO forces in the North Atlantic. You will be riding DICKSON, so take your sea bag over there and report to their executive officer for assignment to quarters and joining the mess. There will be a meeting of my staff here at 0800 tomorrow and we will take care of formalities then." He extended his hand with "Glad to have you aboard, Padre, you have a big pair of boots to fill." "I'm happy to be aboard sir, and for the record, I brought my own boots." We held each other's gaze in freeze frame, then I came to attention, turned and departed.

"Joining the mess" would be a new experience for me. Officers aboard Navy ships do not eat in the same place or the same food as the crew, but join the Officers' Mess, an established co-op in which each officer purchases a share of the net worth then gets billed monthly for his share of the food. The meals are served by enlisted men called stewards. Officers eat in the wardroom, a combination dining room, meeting room and lounge, a place to rest, play cards, watch a movie and socialize. There was always fresh coffee on the sideboard and a steward to serve it.

Back on the pier we exchanged salutes and Charlie spoke the traditional seaman's farewell, "Fair winds and following seas", saluted and turned about face. Like that, I was now Staff Chaplain, DESRON TWELVE. I was the spiritual leader of over two thousand men who were distributed in eight ships and some dozen or more religious backgrounds, or none. I picked up my bag, located hull number 708 and boarded USS HARLAN R. DICKSON, my new temporary home. I sensed that this was the "real Navy". I met Dickson's Executive Officer, (X.O.) second in command of the vessel who was also president of the mess.(The ship's captain eats alone.) He greeted me briefly, assigned me to the upper bunk in forward officers' quarters, said he would see me at dinner and introduced me to the other ship's officers. "Forward officers' quarters turned out to be a cubicle below decks reached by a near-vertical steel ladder to a tiny compartment directly under one of the five inch gun mounts. There were upper and lower bunks, a shared steel desk-chest-cabinet-locker with the gunnery officer. A small steel sink completed the 8'X10' suite. In a flashback to the private staterooms that I occupied in GAFFEY and SERPENT gave me a moment's pause.

George, who would be my roommate, was on leave and had

claimed the lower bunk, so I stripped to my underwear and climbed into the upper noting that my nose was about one foot below the steel deck above. I relaxed, consciously releasing the tension of the day. The inner voice began its questioning again. "What am I doing here? Is this what I asked for? How will I make good the smart-ass comeback to the Commodore? Will the repeat-recycle pass for ministry on this man-o-war? Will I be measured by Charlie's programs and style? I drifted off to sleep with surreal nightmares of what was to come. Perhaps I was cut out for Beaver Creek after all. The hum of the ship's machinery woke me in a sweat. I found a shower across the passageway, bathed, shaved, and put on a clean uniform. Hungry, I set out to find the wardroom.

I entered thee wardroom to a table set for eight, linen table cloth and napkins and half a dozen young officers standing and wearing khaki uniforms with ties. The xo (shorthand for executive officer) entered from the opposite side of the room, took his place at the head of the table as the other officers moved to their chairs. The XO waved me to the chair at his left, enacting 200 years of tradition: no one sits until the senior officer sits, then the others from his right by seniority, The XO spoke: "Gentlemen, we have the honor of embarking the new squadron chaplain, Lieutenant Donald Weir. Please make him feel welcome." On that cue stewards in white jackets began serving us, in order of rank, of course.

The XO turned to me and asked, "What is your denomination, Padre?" "I was born, reared, educated and ordained a Presbyterian, but I have evolved into something of a hybrid.".

"How so?"

All other conversation ceased, forks paused midway to mouths and all attention was focused on the Q and A at the head of the table. I felt my stomach muscles tense, my defenses being martialed, but I sensed that this was an ideal opportunity to break from the script that I had been following far too long.

"Sir, I began to realize that I could no longer believe all the words of the creed nor parts of the Bible literally, you know, some of the myths and miracles."

"That sounds pretty radical. So what do you believe and what do you preach?"

I met his gaze, smiled and continued. "Sir, I can't let that pass without an invitation to all present to hear what I preach for yourselves at divine worship zero-nine-hundred Sunday. But not to dodge your question, the many myths, miracles and creeds that have long been accepted as fact and not to be questioned, have now been disproven by science, especially physics and astronomy. But, if I remember correctly Sir, we are on one of the three subjects that are traditionally prohibited in the wardroom; women, politics and religion. So, what are odds for the Red Sox to take the pennant this year?"

"Umm, not too good, I'm afraid. Pass the butter, please."

When he finished eating, the Exec.(X.O.) excused himself and retuned his desk piled with paperwork that I had noted earlier. Two of the youngest-looking officers, each wearing single gold bars on his collar, followed me as I walked outside to the open deck for a smoke. The tall one spoke: "Padre, tell us more about parting ways with the churches that continue to cling to ideas, myths and miracles that science has disproved. We both have engineering degrees, both come from strong religious traditions and have talked about our faith in God but we too are unable to accept all the teachings of the churches.

"What has been your religious experience, Mister... "Hutton, sir, call me Pete. My family is fourth generation Episcopalian, direct from the Church of England. The ritual, the Mass, the language, ceremonies and vestments have a certain beauty but that does not feed my spiritual hunger or fill a spiritual aloneness. No church or preacher has. Your predecessor was a Baptist, Southern Baptist, a fundamentalist-give -your heart to Jesus and save your soul Baptist. I just could not relate to that".

"How about you, Mister..." "Miller, sir, Gale Miller. I was born into a family of born again Methodists who accepted the

Bible as the not-to-be-questioned word of God and who recited the Apostles' Creed without thought or question. I received a football scholarship to an Ivy League school where I majored in humanities and history, reading Emerson, Kant, Descartes, Nietzsche, "The Rise and Fall of the Roman Empire", and Karl Marx. Most of my classmates were avowed agnostics or outright atheists, but something in me always hungered for food of a spiritual dimension , something which would satisfy both my intellect and my soul."

After a pause I replied, "This may sound radical, even heretical to some, but I believe I have the same direct access to God as did Moses and the prophets...and so do you. But we have lost the connection...blockaded/blindsided by the church, by clergy, and traditions. Remember, God spoke to Moses from a burning bush, sending him to Egypt to free the Israelites from slavery. God spoke to Moses again, alone on a mountain top giving him the Ten Commandments. God sent Elijah to Horeb, "the mount of God", to experience a great windstorm and earthquake but only was only in the "sound of sheer silence" did he hear the voice of God. (I Kings 19:11 ff.) Read Emerson, thrown out of his pulpit because he could no longer in conscience serve communion. Read Thoreau who found his religion in the solitary life at Walden Pond.. God spoke to Elijah from the stillness following an earthquake on Mt. Horeb.

God needs no church, no temple, no cathedral, priest nor pope to speak to your spirit needs, no geography, set time, nor ritual. God spoke to Elijah in a small voice following a storm. He spoke to David, the shepherd/psalmist, in the pasture. In the New Testament Nicodemus came to Jesus an night, after "lights out" we would say. God will speak to us here on the steel decks of the DICKSON. So when you lie in your bunks tonight, consciously open your spirit to the Spirit of God. I hear so many prayers that sound like shopping lists for God, our super-errand boy. "Send us rain, heal my nephew, don't let the bank foreclose, make her say yes!). Listen, don't whine, don't give the Almighty a shopping list of wants, and don't try to tell God how bad you feel. Listen. Listen not for a human-like voice for Spirit speaks to spirit in the language of Spirit."

"It is growing late, gentlemen, it has been a long day for me and it's time now explore the amenities of the "Dickson-Hilton". And, by the way, you have just been appointed Dickson lay leaders! Goodnight! I'll see you in church!"

Below decks I shed the uniform, brushed my teeth, and crawled into the upper bunk where I lay staring at the deck plates above, trying to assimilate the day's events, especially the last hour when I broke from the script and spoke from my spontaneously from my heart and revealed my true beliefs openly. The admonition of the professor who counseled, "Give your testimony" I had taken to mean the only testimony I had heard, the emotional, tearful and public confessions of sins that I had never personally experienced. But, in the last two hours, I had unawares given my testimony, shared openly how God had spoken to me as he had Elijah, in a "still small voice", following a storm. God had spoken to me in the pasture, in the whistle of the gopher and the song of the meadowlark. I remembered handing a bar of soap to the barefoot Vietnamese mother with her baby slung to her breast. I thought of the two young officers who were attracted to my few impromptu words, curious about the new kind of chaplain and hungry for a faith that did not argue with science.

chapter seventeen
BORN AGAIN

I awoke Sunday to a sense of calm, a deep peace that I had not before experienced. In the past 24 hours I had put aside the script and spoke spontaneously from my spirit, from my inner truth and it was accepted as authentic faith, and apparently resonated with the needs of at least two officers in DICKSON.

I shaved quickly, put on a clean uniform and headed for the wardroom where I found only the duty officer and two stewards. I introduced myself and presented my napkin ring to the chief steward who then seated me according to rank. As I noted earlier, wardroom tables are covered in linen, each officer having his own napkin, identified with his name or other ID on a napkin ring. These rings were often creatively decorated with insignia of rank, nickname, or position. I have seen them made from 3" brass shell casings, a bamboo stalk, from spent ammunition to beadwork or one's alma mater. Mine bore a petite silver cross soldered on a plain sterling band. I ordered the Navy's traditional Sunday morning breakfast, steak and eggs, no chopped flank steak but a generous cut of choice tenderloin, with corn muffins still warm from the oven. We ate in the near silence of sleepy men just off the early watch.

I finished the meal and took a "coffee to go" and climbed up to the gun tub of mount 51 to observe "Morning Colors" a ceremony as old as the Navy itself. The flags on ships that are at anchor or moored are lowered at sunset and hoisted again at exactly 0800 hours. With 20 some ships moored side-by-side, morning colors are orchestrated by SOPA, senior officer present afloat. Using a P.A. system audible to all ships in the area, SOPA's bugler sounds Attention!, signaling everyone within hearing range, aboard or ashore, to stand at attention. SOPA sounds eight bells, as the national anthem is played, each ship executes "colors" raising the flag at the stern and the union jack at the bow. (The flag is flown on the mainmast only when the vessel is underway.) At the conclusion of the Star Spangled Banner SOPA announces "carry on" at which all persons and activities that had been at attention now return to their duties.

I stayed to observe several ships including Dickson, hoist and two- block the church pennant to the yard arm. The pennant is a long white triangle with a blue cross extending its entire length, indicating that religious services are being held on board. At sea the pennant on the mainmast is flown above the stars and stripes. It is the only signal that is flown above the flag, a tradition that goes back farther than anyone can remember.

Aboard the vessel where church service is held, where the pennant is flying, the 1-MC (read PA system) announces. "Church call! Church call! First Division, rig for Church! Divine worship is being conducted on the mess decks (or fantail, or forward weather deck). All hands keep silent in the vicinity of religious services. The smoking light is out throughout the ship. Church call!"

I shivered involuntarily, feeling a sense of patriotism, a sense of belonging to something larger than myself and a sense of mission, a sense of destiny.

For a homily I decided to repeat the spontaneous remarks I had spoken last night.

My two newly appointed lay leaders had supervised "rigging for church, erecting and securing a portable aluminum altar and lectern, hymnbooks and Bibles, a tape recorded with numerous hymns, and Navy-gray folding chairs. Six Dickson sailors and a few from adjoining ships were present. I proceeded with the standard opening, call to worship, invocation, hymns and prayers.

Then I stood at the lectern and began extemporaneously.

SUNDAY SERMON..."BORN AGAIN"

"Now there was a Pharisee named Nicodemus, a leader of the Jews. He came to Jesus by night and said to him, 'Rabbi, we know that you are a teacher who has come from God; for no one can do these signs that you do apart from the presence of God,. Jesus answered him, 'Very truly, I tell you, no one can see the kingdom of God without being born from above' Nicodemus said to him, 'How can anyone be born after having grown old? Can one enter a second time into the mother's womb and be born?' Jesus answered, 'Very truly I tell you, no one can enter the kingdom of god without being born of water and the spirit. Do not be astonished that I said to you, you must be born from above." (John 3:2ff)

I recently read in a science magazine that at our birth....no, even earlier, at our conception, the very moment that our father's sperm connected to our mother's ovum, that every detail of our makeup was present in that microscopic single cell. Our gender, male or female, the color of our skin, hair and eyes were all in those genes that resided in a single cell. Not only our physical traits but our talents, an ear for music, the athletic physique for sports, or inclinations for science, poetry or law.

While this was not in the article, it is my personal belief that each of us also comes into this world with a mission, a life work and the special talents, gifts to carry out that mission; and happy indeed is the person who makes that discovery early, who connects his talent, with his mission. Think of Thomas Edison, alone in his lab doing hundreds of experiments until he creates the light bulb. Think of Tolstoy who was locked in his library for years to write

War and Peace. Think of those early sea-going men who set sail in unknown waters, warned by both church and science that they would sail off the edge of the earth and perish. But they had an inner- knowing that the world is round, Magellan, Drake, and Cook and their exploits are now history. Think of Beethoven, Mozart, Verdi and Brahms who gave us a legacy of music that inspires us hundreds of years later. They did not copy someone else's ideas. They reached deep into their souls to grasp that talent which God has planted there.

Each one of us here this morning has an array of gifts and talents, some yet undiscovered and unlike anyone on earth.. Often those talents lay undiscovered because there are other forces, other people, strong people, who try to force upon us their ideas of who we are and what we should be doing. Sometimes it is a parent who plans for a son to take over the family business, or fulfill his unfulfilled dreams of becoming a doctor, lawyer, professor or farmer. I believe that this may be what Jesus was talking about to Nicodemus, about being born again, about the time when you must leave home, go into the wilderness (or go to sea) and seek to discover your divine mission on earth. Even Jesus, when he had been baptized, went into the wilderness for forty days before beginning his ministry to connect with his Father. Now, right here, this morning and the coming days at sea, you also may connect with God and discover God's purpose in your life. It need not be at a worship service, but anytime; as you crawl into your bunk at night, on the midwatch, as you go about your duties, God is present with you, Listen.! Open your hearts and your minds and listen.

Some of you know that the New Testament was written in Greek many years before it was translated into English and that there is more than one way to translate a word. The Greek word "pneuma" is most often translated "spirit", but it can be translated "air", "breath" or "wind". You mechanics will recognize with pneumatic tools.

You medics will recognize it in pneumonia. I like to think that the New Testament use of "pneuma" is "breath" , thus literally the Bible invites us to breathe in the breath of God. Does anyone here remember the old gospel hymn: "Breath on me breath of God, fill me with life anew.........". So, I invite you in God's name, as you say your evening prayers, or when you have a quiet moment anywhere, to be conscious of the presence of God, spirit of God, of the breath of God and breath in the very Spirit of God, breathe out any cares, and sorrows and breathe in the Spirit of God.

And may the peace of God fill your hearts and minds. Amen.
# # #

As Father McQuaid had promised, we were underway at 0700 Monday, steaming out of Narragansett Bay into the Atlantic Ocean. The North Atlantic lived up to its reputation with gale force winds, giant waves spilling green water over the Dickson's bridge. Lifelines on the main deck were carried away. Everything inside that was not secured was flung wildly about, dishes, ash trays, books, shoes and tools. I was sick. I was scared. I felt like Jonah being punished for fleeing from God's mission, but when the skies eventually cleared and the winds abated we were treated to a magnificent display of the Northern Lights evoking awe and wonder at their beauty. It was much like seeing the rainbow after a rainstorm, times ten.

For the next two years I was embarked in each ship several times, often transferring between ships while in foreign ports, sometimes at sea or back in Newport. The squadron proudly accepted the sobriquet "The Steaming Demons" reflecting the months we spent at sea. During the 23 months of this duty we made three trips to Europe, the first mentioned above took us to Scotland and England. Next came a seven month deployment to the Mediterranean visiting Naples, Genoa, Cannes, Izmir, Malta and Athens. While in these ports of call I conducted worship for all of the ships present as well as making myself available for counseling and changing my "residence" from one vessel to another. Occasionally we would moor adjacent to ships of other countries and I would visit them, invite a local Catholic priest aboard to say mass, and offer any service the crews might need.

At Christmas 1957, we were moored alongside a British cruiser in Cannes, France, so I invited their crewmembers to Christmas services aboard PURDY and several attended. One of the Brits stayed afterword to ask briskly, "What's with all the "Thees" and "Thous" and "Thy's?" That was the first time I realized that all of my life I had been addressing the Almighty in King James English. It was not only me, but it was all that I had ever heard anyone use, not only in prayer but in hymns and the liturgies for weddings, funerals and the sacraments. I began talking to God in daily English but found that my mind and tongue were not easily retrained, and my mind pictured a "The Big Guy in the Sky", our Father in heaven. Is this one reason the un-churched, the young people felt no connection with or attraction to the obscure liturgies of Midwestern fundamentalism couched in the obscure vocabularies of the 17th century? How many other antiquated terms and practices was I using that could be translated into present day usage? Now that I had learned and taught communication by spirit, by breath, the larger question remained, do we need language at all when we pray. The Bible had been translated into several contemporary idiomatic versions that were being widely accepted. The discovery and translations of the Dead Sea Scrolls and other ancient manuscripts that pre-dated those used by the King James translators brought forth more accurate meanings of Scripture. Scholars now argued the meanings of words, meanings that had long been accepted without question. How can I take the words of Isaiah, David, Jesus, or Matthew and relate them in terms that the youth culture of the day can understand? My mind began to think of God, less of a person and more like Paul Tillich's "ground of our being" and Ralph Waldo Emerson's "Oversoul". (footnote: the universal mind or spirit that animates, motivates and is the unifying principle of all living things.)

A newer question began to work its way out of the unconscious. "Why was the Bible accepted as the infallible word of God? Why did the words that God supposedly spoke to Moses, Solomon, and the prophets a few thousand years ago relate to 20th century men manning a two thousand ton warship practicing for war? Why was not the word that God speaks to me as valid as the words recorded in Deuteronomy, which had suffered through several translations and versions? After all, had not Martin Luther, firebrand of the Protestant Reformation proclaimed "the priesthood of all believers". "Every man his own priest" was one mantra of the Great Reformation", so am I not empowered to speak the word of God to my generation as the great reformers did to theirs? How can the words of Moses the sheep herder who thought the world was flat, who could not imagine an automobile, airplane, radio or telephone speak to gunner's mate on a destroyer equipped with radar?

As a newly "born again" I was learning that God's word to me was as authentic as those spoken to the prophets, not to be thrust on to others but to teach others to listen for and hear God's word to them. On that same trip in the Mediterranean we visited Turkey, Greece, and Malta for supplies and some sightseeing. Other ports on other trips included Glasgow, Plymouth, Rotterdam, Bergen, Kiel and more. Each gave me a broader understanding of people of other traditions, other religions, as I was often being hosted by local clergy or military chaplains of the armed forces of other countries. In each country I visited the great churches and cathedrals, masterpieces of architecture, many supported by government funds but largely considered by the citizens to be irrelevant to their lives and unattended. These relics of formers ages and cultures with their elaborate furnishings and liturgies were unused except for official ceremonies and royal weddings. The practices of yoga, transcendental meditations and new age and other movements sprang up in their place. Each of these observations and experiences raised new questions about my faith. Each chipped away at the traditions in which I was educated and ordained. Each added to the questions raised while evacuating the refugees in Viet Nam years earlier.

The Navy's promise to see the world was delivered in spades. I toured villages and churches and cities that were heavily bombed by allied forces at a terrible loss of life and property. I attended the ballet in Amsterdam, the opera in Naples, Edward Grieg's home near Bergen, the fabled canals of Venice, the catacombs of Malta, the Parthenon in Athens, and the Biblical site in Ephesus. The languages, dress, customs, food and housing were different in each place, but the people were working to better themselves, worshipping in strange modes and celebrating holidays unknown to me. Then there were the days at sea with time to reflect and absorb these experiences and weigh them against our language, our religions, experience and culture. What do we have in common? What divides us? What does the rapid communication via TV, radio, air travel in the future, bode for our relations with these people? And still to be discovered was the internet and social media.

Even though I lived elbow to elbow with the crews of my ships, they largely ignored the religious services, save for those few with strong religious convictions and who found some comfort in the Scriptures, hymns and sacraments. There were unexpected benefits of those days and weeks at sea; while the crews of the ships were busily engaged in drills simulating combat conditions, anti-aircraft and surface gunnery, locating and depth charging submarines, fighting fires and caring for the dead and wounded, I had time to read, write and reflect.

"Pastoral Counseling", a seminary text book, mostly unread, introduced me to "non-directive counseling", a practice based on the theories developed by the noted psycho-therapist, Carl Rogers. Rogers and Hiltner taught that the counselors' role was not to solve the clients' problems, but through non-directive, open end questions, assist the client to clarify his problem and discover the solutions from within. This was a "light bulb experience for me. I began to practice these methods and have used them these many years with very satisfactory results as I saw myself not as a "problem solver" but a facilitator assisting people in finding and adopting happy life changes.

But the most significant event of those two years was meeting and marrying a beautiful young lady from Newport, homeport of the Acey Deucy squadron. Both she and her family accepted me just as I was, no role playing, no pretending, just the farm boy in uniform trying to find my life's mission. They were third generation Newporters, nominally Christian, Easter and Christmas church goers, generous and genial people who welcomed me to their home and treated me as family, that I became. Fifty-five years later we are still married with children, grandchildren and a great-grandson.

Mom, I was sorry you could not attend the wedding due to Dad's heart attack, but it was great to have you visit in the summer of 1959, to give you your first look at the Atlantic Ocean, drive up to Cape Cod, introduce you to fresh lobster and clam chowder and take you, Dad, aboard a Navy ship for lunch. I still wear the watch that I gave you at that time. I am sure that you felt the gulf between my life, my changing values and yours, but you held your peace. Thank you.

Mom and Dad: We rarely saw each other in the 1960s, years that ushered in "The New Age", years in which I was questioning many of the teaching and beliefs of our faith, while seeking ways to bring faith in God to young people who could not relate to the traditional language and trappings of the Church.

chapter eighteen
A NEW AGE DAWNS

Say "The Sixties" to anyone of us alive during those years and we recall images of Rock and Roll bands, Hippies, Woodstock, encounter groups, marijuana, LSD, and communal living. We remember the Beatles and Elvis. We remember young men burning draft cards, anti-war protests, and draft- dodgers fleeing to Canada. "New Age" was not an organized movement, but a term that embraced new and alternative life styles, group living, pop-psychology and the use of mind-altering drugs. "Tune in and drop out", the new-agers called out at anti-war rallies where they burned the American flag and demonstrators carried hand painted signs with anti-establishment slogans. Timothy Leary, Harvard professor. was experimenting with LSD and other mind-altering drugs; Leary's colleague, Richard Alpert, studied Eastern religions in India and returned as a Hindu, "Ram Dass" and whose teachings inspired many Americans, young and not so young, to turn to Eastern thought and practices. These were the intellectuals voicing these changes. Sigmund Freud, granddaddy of psychotherapy, was being replaced by new schools of psychology pioneered by Abraham Maslow, Carl Rogers, Carl Jung and Fritz Perls who was known as the father of gestalt psychotherapy. At Big Sur, California, the Esalen Institute was the best known of many personal growth centers, employing new group psychologies, encounter groups, or T-Groups. It was a time of casting off traditional living patterns (and often clothing) and experimenting with new life styles. The term "Human Potential Movement" was coined as an umbrella term for these activities. Abraham Maslow's writings and teaching of humanistic psychology strongly influenced the social science community to re-think their understanding of human nature, some were blending psychology and spirituality. Self-help groups, T-Groups, and even martial arts were gaining popularity.

Some Christian seminaries began increasing the emphasis on pastoral care and counseling, studying a new breed of psychologists such as Carl Rogers and Carl Jung. Theological curriculums now included "Clinical Pastoral Education" with requirements for residency in hospitals and mental health institutions.

During these tumultuous years I had been had been physically and militarily isolated from much of the drama of the New Age. My family and I had been living overseas or I had been at sea. The career Navy officers with whom I served considered most New Age activities at best unpatriotic and at worst treasonous. They soundly condemned flag burning, draft card burning, and fleeing the country. Some of my attempts to update worship or express sympathy anti-war activities were given short shrift and looked upon with disdain and considered "new-agey".

Early in 1968 I was ordered to sea again, this time in USS CANBERRA home ported in San Diego. The young sailors of CANBERRA, however, had been deeply influenced by rock and roll music, the rallies and events making up the culture of the New Age. Use of marijuana and other mind altering substances was growing. This culture was creeping into the Navy and other branches of the Armed Forces, shaking the foundations of two hundred years of military traditions of discipline and good order.

The youngest of CANBERRA's crew were most deeply

attracted to rock and roll, the use of cannabis and antiwar activities. Some young men who were considering "jumping ship" and fleeing to Canada came to me for counseling, torn between their enlistment oath and a conscience that strongly opposed the war and serving on this warship. They were scorned as "peaceniks" and they in turn considered others as "warmongers", I could only help them clarify their options and the consequences of each. I shared many of their quandaries between taking a stand for the sanctity of life and my oath to "support and defend the Constitution of the United States of America and to obey such orders the President may issue from time.". The following episode illustrates my dilemma.

We sailed for WESTPAC (the western Pacific area of operations) without several crew members. I sailed with a heavy heart, both for leaving my young family to care for themselves in a strange city, and for field of combat that lay ahead.

It was in CANBERRA, cruising off the coast of "enemy territory", that the Admiral invited me to his private dining room for dinner. "Padre, what do you think of what's going on out here?" he asked. "Admiral, I am proud of my country and proud to wear this uniform, but I am also a servant of the One called 'Prince of Peace", the One who taught us to love our enemies. So I feel squeezed between a rock and a hard place. I have not been able to reconcile these two loves." He changed the subject.

Meanwhile I continued to play a balancing act, following the script written by church and military, and reaching out to those who also felt torn between military oaths and an inner truth, who opposed the war and embraced the new age. I tried to see myself as the mediator, the bridge between the traditional expressions of both religious faith and patriotism and the new age that was being born before my eyes. Late in 1969 Canberra was "mothballed", Navy slang for decommissioned and transferred to the reserve fleet. It was stripped of ammunition, armaments and equipment that could be salvaged for use elsewhere. It would eventually be sold for scrap.

I had received orders to attend the "Advanced Course" at the Navy Chaplain School, Newport, RI. We welcomed this move across country where we would live walking distance to Bev's parents, grandparents of our children, Diane 9, Dave, not yet 5. The trip across country also included a December stop in Windom to visit my family and allow our kids to play in their first snow.

Mom and Dad, we enjoyed visiting you in Windom, seeing you and friends. Diane and Dave loved their introduction to snow. Thanks for the warm reception and Mom's home cooking. We also always loved having you visit us, especially when it involved those long tr0ips to San Diego, D.C. and Newport.

The Senior Course's original purpose was to prepare chaplains in the rank of commander for supervisory duties on large military installations, including the supervision of several chaplains of other faiths and traditions. It was considered a mandatory step up towards the next promotion. When the course convened we learned that it also incorporated in the curriculum intense study of the "New Age", of the music and the life style of the young men and women in the Navy, and develop new forms of ministries, more relevant to many who had embraced many of the tenets of the New Age, and to "re-package" our ministries in forms that would appeal to their tastes in music, including participative liturgies, presented in contemporary language and music. We explored forms of meditation, encounter groups, and we sang along with Simon and Garfunkel: "When times get rough and friends just can't be found, like a bridge over troubled water I will lay me down". We visited local churches that were experimenting by replacing pipe organs with guitars, drums, and harmonicas. My classmates had mixed reactions to these experiences, some felt threatened and some welcomed them as a sign of hope for the future and as vehicles and a bridge between eternal truth and present reality. I embraced these changes as vehicles for the changes I had been experiencing, relating my beliefs to this generation of young sailors.

Much of the course was not classroom lecture and discussion, but physical immersion in the culture of the young people we would be serving. In the evenings we went to the clubs where their music was being played, to observe new forms of dancing, to talk with them about what we were seeing and hearing. The class also made week-end retreats where gurus of the new age were present to teach group meditation, encounter groups and other counseling methods. TM, transcendental meditation, was a national buzzword. Young adults spoke to us about why they had left the church and why they believed that much of organized religion was irrelevant to their lives, and where they were finding spiritual food for their journeys.

We were assigned readings such as Bishop J. R. Robinson's, "Honest to God" and the cover story of Time Magazine April 8, 1966, 'IS GOD DEAD?' These two were but samples of music, literature and the arts that were challenging traditional religious doctrines and practices. Some of us finished that course determined to present our faith in a language that would speak to the young men and women who would make up our next "flocks", teens in uniform. My mind and my notebook were filled with ideas and programs to implement at my next duty and I was thrilled when orders to Naval Training Command, Orlando, Florida arrived.

The six month's stay in Newport had been invigorating for the family. Bev enjoyed good times with her parents. Diane, 10 and David 3 experienced more snowballs and snowmen and their doting grandparents' affection. The moving van rolled up and swallowed our furniture as we loaded the station wagon with kids, dog, toys and snacks and headed for Orlando, Florida.

chapter nineteen

NAVAL TRAINING CENTER ORLANDO, FLORIDA 1970–1975

Mom and Dad, I doubt that the New Age had much effect on life in Windom, but it definitely changed my world view, my way of thinking and gave me the tools to help young men and women discover their talents, their beliefs and for their future. It changed my life and gave form to ideas that had been nascent for years. But the New Age surely increased the cultural distance between us.

The Naval Training Center was comprised of several subordinate commands, schools to teach specialized trades and skills.. Its several hundred acres were dotted with modern brick buildings that housed schools for recruit training, schools for torpedo men, electronics technicians, clerical ratings, and the largest of all, Recruit Training Command where thousands of raw recruits, fresh from the New Age culture and the backwoods of West Virginia were thrust overnight into the rigid routines of basic training; Boot Camp! It was my good fortune to be assigned as Senior Chaplain of recruit training with a large contemporary chapel and a staff of several junior chaplains.

I was immediately assigned as the senior chaplain at RTC with four other chaplains working with me. All the buildings at RTC were new brick construction, barracks for several hundred recruits, training buildings with multiple classrooms, medical and dental facilities and a beautiful new chapel of contemporary design, featuring semi-circular seating with floor sloping forward, theater style and facing a beautiful gold-anodized reredos. Comfortable offices for the chaplains, a sacristy, baptistery, and small chapels for daily mass and Jewish services provided a dramatic contrast to a temporary altar rigged on the mess decks of a destroyer while navigating the stormy waters of the North Atlantic in October!

The mission of RTC was to transform civilian youth coming from a culture of rock and roll, free love, marijuana and counter-culture drop-outs into disciplined, motivated fighting men in twelve weeks. The moment the recruits entered the base they were stripped of their jewelry, tie-dyed clothing, and "Jesus sandals" and had their shoulder-length hair clipped tight to the scalp. Now clothed in regulation Navy dungarees, chambray shirts, baseball caps and "clodhopper" work shoes, drill instructors constantly shouted in their faces and they were not allowed to speak without permission and moved from place to place only in formation and in step with 75 other bewildered youth to a cadence called by their drill instructors, senior enlisted men with years of service.

The recruits were given inoculations, medical and dental exams, and several classes daily on such subjects as military history, seamanship, personal hygiene and character guidance.

They marched! They marched to breakfast. They marched from class to class. They marched to lunch. Then they marched to the drill field, the "grinder" where they were taught to march. In the evenings they hand-washed their own clothing, cleaned the barracks and heads (bathrooms). They went to bed at taps, 2100 hours, "lights out" and were awakened with reveille at 0500. After a few days of this routine, many recruits experienced "culture shock,", a mental state of disorientation, despair and depression. They had left the supportive culture of parents, girlfriends, buddies, music, dances, TV, snacks, soft drinks and doing much as they pleased when they pleased. Now their lives were under complete control of the U. S. Navy, channeled through their drill instructor, the D.I. There was no sleeping-in, no snooze alarm, no freedom, and no spare time.

It was into this milieu that I stepped from the casual, civilian attired senior course at Chaplains School. I remember the first Sunday in Recruit Chapel. I sat in the back and observed the chaplain I was to relieve demonstrate the "approved" method of leading recruits in worship. Suddenly the doors were opened and 800 dungaree-clad, downcast, depressed young men filed in, standing at attention until seated by their D.I. with the admonition to "keep quiet". The chaplain appeared in the pulpit and conducted the typical stereotype service found in any conservative Protestant church. The recruits sat in stone faced silence, occasionally mumbling printed responses and gospel hymns. When the benediction was pronounced they sang "Eternal Father", the Navy hymn, a signal for the D. I.s who had been outside smoking, to open the doors, enter and call attention. The recruits were then marched back to their barracks with the usual amount of shouting to keep in step, square the hats and keep their eyes forward.

I thought, I don't know what I'm going to do here, but I am NOT going to do that! With the full support and encouragement of Ed Hemphill, my boss, I bought some guitars, tambourines, a harmonica and drums, and then put out a call to the recruits for volunteers who would like to play and sing for chapel services. I was overwhelmed with the flood of talent that came forward and the enthusiasm with which they helped put together a new service. A guitarist who had had his own rock band before enlisting, a jazz pianist and soul-singer with night club experience, a country music guitarist and singer, an organist with a master's degree in music, a drummer who had played with a nationally recognized group, and a group of six "soul brothers" who sang the closest harmony I had ever heard. While rehearsals were in progress, I arranged for all D.I.s and other non-recruit personnel to stay outside the chapel during services.

The following Sunday the prelude was "Joy to the World", not the Christmas carol but the Three Dog Night's: "Jeremiah was a bull frog, a very good friend of mine...............", belted out and amplified through an outstanding sound system. The troops came out of their seats, clapping, swaying and singing along to the music of one of their songs after another: "The Impossible Dream", "Bridge over Troubled Waters", "What the World Needs Now is Love, Sweet Love" "You've Got a Friend", and "Leaving on a Jet Plane". All recruits attended church in working clothes, dungarees, chambray shirts, boots and baseball caps. Graduating recruits, those who, celebrating their final Sunday, wore their dress whites, referred to as their "Cracker Jacks", and were seated in the very front rows. When it was time for prayer, instead of praying for them to become good sailors for God and country as did my predecessor, I asked them to stand, one at a time and briefly pray aloud. They responded with an outpouring of concerns for their families, for each other, for brothers on the front lines in Viet Nam and for strength to make it through another day of training. Most moving of all were the prayers of those graduating recruits, their final Sunday in training, praying encouragement for those in their first and second weeks of deep culture shock. During the "passing of the peace" these same senior recruits stepped out of their coveted seats and into the aisles, found the most depressed looking first week recruits and embraced and encouraged them, assuring them that they too would survive and soon be celebrating in those front rows. I don't remember my "sermon", only that it was brief, assuring them that God is with us not only in good times, but in tough times as well illustrated in the lives of the prophets, the saints and Jesus, himself.

At the conclusion of the service, instead of marching, heads down, they were dancing out the chapel doors, affirmed in their self-worth and self-esteem, bathed in mutual support and the love of God. As a result, I spent more than one Monday morning in the C.O.'s office explaining why the troops were dancing out of the chapel and why I was undermining the discipline that they were working so hard to instill. But we continued, composing and inventing this new liturgy as we went. We attracted attention beyond Orlando and began receiving inquiries and visits from other commands that heard about the celebrations in Recruit Chapel. In fairness, not all recruits appreciated these new services, and some recruits from very fundamentalist families and traditions were offended, so we continued to offer a traditional service for them. And some guys went to both! It was here that I began to understand worship as a celebration of life, and to understand ministry as creating an enabling experience for these recruits to find their inner truth and connect it with the universal life, to join their spirit with the Universal Spirit, God.

Three years of this ministry had established "Contemporary Worship" as one of several options for the recruits of all faiths. Now other chaplains had been trained in these new modes of worship and were encouraged to bring their own unique ideas and visions to this work.

I was reassigned to SSC, School Command, and asked to develop a religious program relevant to the needs of these students. SSC consisted of several schools, each to teach newly graduated recruits the skills required for specific ratings, their first steps towards a Navy career. Torpedoman's School, Signalman's School taught Morse code, signal flags and flashing light communications, Yeoman's school taught clerical work, producing and managing correspondence, directives and filing. A few months later the Nuclear Power School would open and bring students with high academic ability to study math, physics and nuclear propulsion. Unlike recruit training there were no taps, no reveille, only scheduled classes and assignments. No religious program existed in Service School Command. Students could attend the NTC Chapel where very traditional worship was offered and which was attended by many retired and other older people. Students could seek out civilian churches, but few did. These were 18-23 year old men and women whose civilian contemporaries were burning draft cards, protesting the war in Viet Nam, smoking pot, hitch-hiking across the country to rock concerts and experimenting with a variety of communal living arrangements. Most of the students ignored any form of religious activity and found some relief in listening to rock and roll and drinking beer on the week-ends. I did not know where to begin working with these students. I had no pre-packaged, one-size-fits-all program and I needed a break from three years at RTC, I asked for and was granted "Temporary Orders for Training" with University Associates' a civilian training organization whose clients included top leaders in the country's major corporations and institutions. I enrolled in a ten day program in two parts: first, personal development that employed T-group sessions, self-disclosure and group feedback, and part two presented ways to initiate change in an organization.

I was one of twelve enrolled in a ten day course of intensive self-assessment and planning, one in a group of twelve executives, teachers, managers and other professionals. I was the only clergy and the only military presence. This would prove to be another tipping point in my life. In a non-judgmental climate of total acceptance I was encouraged to expose and resolve the inner conflicts which had been raging in my mind for years. The group accepted all this without judgment. They affirmed both my struggles and my talents and offered unconditional acceptance and encouragement to trust my instincts and to create a new and relevant ministry where there had been none.

Here for the first time in my life I experienced the power of structured group experiences, guided imagery and meditation where I was encouraged and enabled to express my deepest feelings and beliefs and have them affirmed by peers. Here were no creeds or catechism, no "shoulds" or "shames", but acceptance of my authentic self, hidden for years while trying to live someone else's script. Listening to other participants wrestle with their doubts, fears and hopes I realized that I was not some freak, but that others shared the struggle to find their gifts and their true mission in life.

The second phase presented the latest thinking of organization development where much of the self-discovery was applied in theoretical board rooms and work groups within real organizations with defined problems to solve. There was much role-playing and problem solving exercises. As we moved through these exercises I experienced a new confidence in my abilities and armed with the tools to develop a program for the new assignment.

The Service School Command consisted of several schools to provide training for specific jobs in the fleet, the first step on a Navy career path. The yeoman's school trained for clerical work, producing and managing the correspondence, directives and filing. The signalman's school taught Morse code, radio communications flashing light and signal flags. Torpedoman's school taught the assembly, servicing and firing torpedoes and depth charges. A few months later the Nuclear Power School was established with a flood of new personnel with high academic ability, here to study math, physics and nuclear propulsion. The high demands of these schools required much night and week-end study, creating much mental pressure and stress for the students. My mandate was to develop a religious program to meet the unique needs of these young, stressed sailors. The only religious service on the base was the old white frame chapel built by years ago the Air Force and now attended by a few base personnel and many retired military and other old people. The protestant service was a traditional conservative event that appealed to the older people. Most of the Service School students had no interest in this service, Bible study and the like. My students largely ignored the chapel, found some relief in Saturday night drinking beer and listening to rock and roll.

I had no pre-packaged, one-size-fits-all religion or program to bring to these bright but highly-stressed men and women. Instead I began to get acquainted, to listen to their hopes and fears, their problems, their feelings and stressors. I "hung out" at the "gedunks" (snack bars) and other gathering places where they discuss their concerns, their lives. I arranged to have a few minutes in some of their classrooms to introduce myself and announce hours for personal counseling and religious services. On a couple of occasions I appeared just before an exam. The tension and stress in the room was written all over their faces. I took a deep breath...and a big chance...and asked them to participate in some simple stress reducing exercises right there on the spot, breathing, visualization, and calming activities. It took only a few minutes but the results were immediately evident. Much o the facial tension was dissolved, scowls and frowns were relaxed , and most of them scored well on the exam. The word soon got around and instructors were calling me to appear at exam time and repeat these exercises.

As I worked with these young people both in the classroom and in personal counseling, I sensed that many were really searching for a personal identity. They had gone from the control of parents, church, and school into the control of the Navy and they had many conflicting thoughts, ideas and feelings about themselves, the purpose of their lives and their future. I began developing a program that became known as "Personal Growth Week-ends".

The town of New Smyrna Beach lies about 100 miles east of Orlando directly facing the Atlantic Ocean. Just one block off the ocean the Methodist church owned a cottage used for retreats. This little three bedroom home was sparsely furnished with bunk beds, a kitchen with appliances and a living room suitable for group activities. We were able to negotiate the use of this place for a week end to launch the first "Personal Growth Weekend". We had no funds for transportation, so I proceeded to pass the exam for a commercial driver's license, then checked out a twenty passenger Navy bus on Friday afternoon, drove by the commissary to load lots of groceries, embarked a dozen of these students, mostly strangers to each other, and then headed for the beach where some of the group would have their first ever view of salt water. Our first order of business was to properly "baptize" these landlubbers by tossing them fully clothed into the surf . That "broke the ice" and began shaping twelve strangers into a group. After showers, unpacking and making up bunks we attacked the groceries, mostly heat-and-eat items, then settled into 48 hours of intensive group encounter. In an atmosphere of mutual trust and confidentiality the event was designed to facilitate self-disclosure, peer feedback, affirmation and support using structured experience, group discussions, guided imagery and meditation. The response to the weekend was enthusiastic. Many of these young men and women for the first time in their lives felt free to reveal their inner hopes, dreams, and fears, felt understood, listened to, accepted and affirmed, often in tears, hugs and laughter. The twelve apprehensive and anxious sailors who left Orlando on Friday headed back late Sunday, celebrating their experience with singing, laughing and mutual affirmations. By Monday morning word of their experience had spread through their barracks, and the next "weekends" were quickly subscribed and had waiting lists. With my time there growing short, I trained other chaplains to continue the work.

The further I moved away from traditional forms of worship and from the doctrines into which I was born and trained, the more authentic I felt about myself and my ministry. When homosexual people openly and publically announce their sexual orientation, they use the term, "coming out of the closet". This is how I felt as I quit playing the orthodox roles of my ordination, and openly declared that I no longer believed all of the creeds, catechisms and sacraments that had accumulated around the teaching of Jesus as found in the gospel stories. I denied the belief that celibacy is a more noble way of life than marriage, and denounced the belief that the hierarchy of the clergy has the power and authority to forgive sins; to excommunicate and literally "send to hell" is both repugnant and untenable. Why do millions of otherwise sane and rational people enter the confessional, whisper their sins to the priest, receive absolution and are assigned recitation of two "our Fathers" and six "Hail Marys" as penance? Secretly I asked why Moses or Isaiah had more access to God than anyone of us. I reasoned that every civilization of the past had its gods and its religions. The Canaanites had their Baal, Greeks had their Ares and Dionysus, the Romans, Jupiter, Mars and Saturn and the Norse worshipped Odin, Mars and Thor. Tribes in the remote jungles of Africa and South America and the Native North America, gazed at the sun, moon, stars, planets and attributed names of gods to them, offered them sacrifices, ceremonies and prayers.

Today we have a growing body of scientific information about the universe. Giant telescopes are revealing not only the secrets of our universe but the existence of galaxies beyond galaxies that stretch our minds and our imaginations beyond "Our Father". As I articulated these thoughts I found myself in the company of great thinkers such as the American transcendentalist Emerson who spoke of the deity as the "Oversoul". (footnote: the universal mind or spirit that animates, motivates and is the unifying principle of all living things.), and was dismissed from his church for his ideas and for refusing to serve the sacrament of Holy Communion. Fellow chaplains of traditional and conservative beliefs distanced themselves from me and some senior chaplains seemed threatened by these new ministries which they did not understand or control and found heretical and, who I later found, had blocked my promotion. Big change was coming. I was about to step out of the box "big time".

I was notified in early 1975 that I would not be selected for promotion to captain and that I would be retired on June 30 that year. I was disappointed, but not surprised or dismayed and set about planning a new life as a civilian.

> "What is it in man that for a long while lies unknown and unseen only one day to emerge and push him into a new land of the eye, a new region of the mind, a place he has never dreamed of? Maybe it's like the force of spores lying quietly under asphalt until the day they push a soft, bulbous mushroom head right through the pavement. There's nothing you can do to stop it."
>
> William Least Heat Moon
> "Blue Highways p. 162

"It's never too late to be what you might have been."

George Eliot

"If there is one thing that has made a difference in my life,
it is the courage to turn and face what
wants to change within me."

Elizabeth Lesser "Broken Open" p.19

chapter twenty
RETIREMENT RETURN
TO CIVILIAN LIFE

Mom and Dad,

You were silent when you learned that I would not be returning to the Midwest and doing what ministers are "supposed to do", but you held your peace, no doubt wondering what was happening to their second-born son. Jim lived in the home town, now a mail carrier, father of two, director of the choir and soloist for funerals. Emmy, employed at the University, married with two fine sons. But Donnie was still on some mysterious, unconventional, *unpredictable path. What next? What next indeed!"*

hat to do? Where to go? Someone else had answered those questions for twenty years but now it was our decision. We loved San Diego, the climate, the pace of life, the ocean and desert and mountains, but we did not want to leave our Maitland home where Diane and David were in school. Diane, 15, had been in four schools and we were reluctant to move her again. There were no United Presbyterian clergy jobs in central Florida; anyhow, I would no longer fit the expectations of such positions. I finally recognized that the time had come to listen to the inner voice that had been silenced for a lifetime, time to dismiss the voices of "should". For years I had preached one essential message that I believed, that we each come to earth with a special mission and that we are born with the tools to carry out that mission. I had failed to heed my own sermon. I had given control of my life to others. Now at age 47, I was at a major crossroads, a major opportunity for major change. Is this the much-discussed mid-life crisis I wondered.

Years later I would discover strong affirmation for my decisions in Karen Armstrong's memoir, "The Spiral Staircase": I read and re-read her account of leaving the convent. She wrote:.

"Like so many of Tennyson's people, I too longed to join in the vibrant life that was going all around me, but found myself compelled to withdraw by forces that I did not understand." P. 91

"I erected a barricade of words and wit around myself, so that nobody could see how needy I really was." P. 93 "Did I really believe that there was a Being up there somehow responsible for everything that happens on earth, including Jacob's disabilities? No, I did not. Not only did it seem highly unlikely that there was an overseeing deity, supervising earthly events, apportioning trials and rewards according to some inscrutable program of his own, but the ideas was also grotesque. If there were a loving providence, it bore no relation to any kind of love that I could conceive. I did not believe that this God existed, and as I sat that night beside Jacob in the semidarkness, I wondered if I ever really had." p.111

"I couldn't make religion work for me," I explained." I really tried. I tried to pray, to meditate, but I didn't get anywhere. Oh yes, I know the ritual was wonderful....I remember how much it meant to you....but don't you see? That was just an aesthetic response. 'The real test is when you try to find God on your own, without props, without beautiful music, singing, and spectacle... when there is just you on your knees. And I could never do that."

"Have you lost your faith, then?" Jane asked sharply?

"I don't know that I ever had any faith, not true faith. I wanted to believe it all; I wanted to have an encounter with God. But I never did. God was never a reality for me, never a genuine presence in my life as he was for the other sisters." " I repeated my new manta: 'We will grieve not, rather find Strength in what lies behind." P.130-1

Armstrong's story was like a benediction on my decision to give up the role of clergy and take up the authentic life of a businessman, a salesman, no less. Not give up my faith, but the institution, the creeds and catechisms, the man-made institution. Confirmation of my decision came in the mailbox. A letter from presbytery read in part, "At our regular Stated Meeting of Presbytery held on May 7, 1983....action was taken to move your name from the 'Inactive List' to a 'Special List" as required of us according to a ruling of the Stated Clerk of General Assembly." I had never heard of a "special list" so I wrote for clarification. I paraphrase the response: You cannot perform any official functions that require ordination until you come crawling for our permission. Their action had come without warning, with no consultation, with no, "how are you doing, Don? What are your plans? How may we help?" They notably failed to note that the "perks" of the senior member of Presbytery now passed to someone else. So be it.

For years a new path had been unconsciously forming in my mind. We had lived in government owned housing in Parris Island and in The Philippines. While in the Philippines I enrolled in a real estate correspondence course in preparation for purchasing a home when we returned to the USA. Here I learned the basic vocabulary and procedures, learned about financing, contracts, insurance and taxes. When we returned in 1962 we bought our first home in Kensington, MD, about three miles from the National Naval Medical Center where I would be working. I loved looking at houses with a well-informed agent and I could understand her as she explained the price, terms and features of each one. I questioned her about financing alternatives, clauses in contracts, taxes and title insurance. Years later as the Navy moved us from place to place we purchased homes in Rhode Island, Florida, San Diego and Florida again. I was exhilarated by these experiences, not only finding a suitable home for the family, but the capital appreciation, tax advantages and profit we experienced as we sold them. In each instance I continued to question the real estate agents we worked with about contracts, titles, and financing. These experiences were laying a foundation for a new career. In my time off during my last year of service in Orlando, I completed the classwork for Florida real estate licensure, passed the state exam and was issued a salesman's license. To practice real estate however I must be employed by a broker. So I read the real estate ads in the daily and Sunday newspaper, visited "open houses" and quizzed the hosting agents and read their literature.

While still in uniform, a casual encounter with Ray Wagstaff, a real estate broker, developed first into a friendship, then a business relationship. We met at a funeral that I conducted for the husband of one of his staff. Ray waited after the service to complement me on the eulogy, then asked me to join him at a nearby coffee shop. I told him of my recent licensure as a real estate salesman and he related that he had recently left a large real estate company to form Epic Realty, his own business, then invited me come by his office to discuss joining his company. We proved to be a good match; both born in 1928, both had teen-age children, and mutual interests. About six months before I retired and began attending his weekly sales meetings, then continued full time after retirement. Under Ray's tutelage I began doing quite well in the business. I worked hard and long hours as I had done most of my life but six months after joining Epic, Ray was snatched from this earth without notice. I asked the heavens, "Why were we given this short time together? Why did he leave a fatherless child and a mourning widow and I was given years of joy with children and spouse?" The company soon changed ownership and I lost my mentor and friend. But I had not lost my appetite for the business.

I served as a pall bearer at Ray's funeral where I was seated next to Jack Ballard, also a pall bearer and another of Ray's good friends. Jack was a partner in Village Realty©, a small, four-partner brokerage firm focused on an upscale market. Jack invited me to interview with his company, was hired and very soon became one of their top producing sales people. Much of my success derived from a continued connection with good friends at the Naval Base, They provided me with information about Navy people moving to and from duty in Orlando. They gave me names and addresses of senior officers who would be moving to Orlando from distant cities and overseas. This was a gold mine for business in a highly competitive market where seasoned agents competed for qualified buyers. I phoned these prospects at once and provided them with extensive information about Orlando, housing options, schools and community services. I gave them my 800 number and urged them to call and ask for additional information. I made reservations for temporary living arrangements and met them on arrival. Our many moves around the country had given me a special empathy with buyers coming from many places, anxious about affordability, about schools for their children, driving distances to work, medical facilities, shopping and churches. I sent detailed information by special delivery and followed up with more phone calls. I had established myself as "their agent" before the competition knew of their coming. I found great satisfaction in working closely with these families, forming friendships that lasted many years after the real estate transactions. Over the years they would refer friends, relatives and associates to me, an ongoing source of business.

Driving around the community with these buyers to demonstrate homes, communities and amenities, our conversations ranged from families, occupations, travels and hobbies. I generally deflected any questions about my previous career as a chaplain and kept the focus on my passengers and their needs. One exception to that practice came when a friend from out of state referred a retired clergy couple to me to purchase a retirement home. They knew my background and she kept bringing up my past, and asking why I would abandon my calling for business, especially a business with questionable reputation. "What a waste of your education and your talent" she declared. I responded that honest dealings with folks who were often highly stressed by parting with their life's savings and changing their entire lifestyle for years to come was to me as holy a calling as laying the weekly harangue on them from the pulpit.

After two years of steady business at Village Realty it was obvious that there was to be no upward movement in the ranks of that tightly held partnership and I was itching to grow. I had passed the state broker exam and qualified to teach Florida State license law. When Watson Realty, a large corporation based in Jacksonville, opened a local office with plans for several more, I joined their ranks and was soon selected and trained to join their management team. I was charged with selecting a site for their second office and recruiting a sales staff , a challenge I relished. I leased space in an office building, designed and contracted to build out the facility with offices for sales staff, and a training room for regular sales meetings and to teach evening licensing classes. I was promoted to vice president. I managed a successful sales office, taught license law and sales training for the entire area. I was sent to other Florida cities to teach Florida License Law thus making Watson's presence felt in places ripe for expansion. I felt fully engaged in this new career, and an enthusiasm for life which had previously evaded me. I had published articles in a national real estate journal, was appointed to positions in the local Board of Realtors and generally recognized and respected in the community. Most of all, I discovered a place in the world where my interests, education and skills and personality were fully engaged, that I was measurably productive and having fun. I was elected president of our Homeowners Association, and called upon to mediate financial disputes between Realtors. A national real estate magazine published my article on training new agents. Bev was employed in a fabric store. Our children were enrolled in a private school. Life was good.

After the Navy retired me I had attended a variety of churches, trying to find a place where I fit in, were I would find others of like minds, where my faith would be nourished, my beliefs affirmed but I never found it. I found affirmation and renewal in nature, in the library of free thinkers' books and journals. I felt whole and complete as I scribbled in my journal at the corner table in a busy coffee shop. I felt connected to the Source of the universe on the seashore at dawn and on a quiet walk in the woods, a boy and his dog in the pasture, alone in the prow of the ship at sunrise, mid ocean; the contemplative life. Everywhere I breathed in the Spirit of

God. Life at a slower pace remained a joy.

In 1980 I was invited to join Winter Park Toastmasters, a club of Toastmasters International. This was a group of about 70 high profile business and professional men, all morning people, who gathered at 7:30 every Friday morning to practice and critique public speaking. Here I became friends with many of the community's leaders: attorneys, physicians, accountants, and business owners. These meetings became one of the highlights of my week, and I learned much more about public speaking from some very polished speakers including Steve Torda, Arnold Howell, Karl Righter, Geordie Allen, Roy Scherer, Larry Kittinger and Dean Fletcher. Over the years I was elected to most of the clubs offices including president. I received numerous trophies for speech contests, both in the club and in regional contests with other clubs in the area. I silently thanked the memories of Vivian Newport and "Prof" Newcomb.

As I approached my 70th birthday I began to notice my memory and other mental faculties begin to decline, and I believed that it put my business, the careers of my sales staff, and our clients in jeopardy. Misquoting a dollar amount or miscalculating a closing statement could cause serious consequences for me, our clients, my staff and the company. Following extensive thought, consultation with employer and trusted friends I decided the time had come to retire to a private and personal life. We were financially secure and in reasonable health, but not ready for a retirement home or the senior citizens organizations.

I felt good about the transition. I was free now to write, to speak, to volunteer for the betterment of our community and to employ my farming skills at improving the landscape and garden of our home. I volunteered with Adult Literacy League as a tutor, as a board member and a fund raising speaker for numerous charitable organizations, appealing for funds to support a variety of charities. Health problems that put me in the hospital a few times terminated the literacy connection, so I volunteered to deliver hot meals to shut-ins, an activity of "Seniors First".

The years of working with young men and women in uniform left me with an ongoing interest in reaching out to young adults in a variety of places. Many of these were in service jobs, just going through rote motions behind the counter in fast food stores, stocking grocery shelves, entry level construction work or bussing tables to earn minimum wage while they searched for more direction and purpose in their lives. I noticed that the public often treated these serviced like fixtures or automatons, rarely speaking a word other than ordering food. I made it a point to speak with these kids, asking about their lives, their hopes for the future and education. Their responses were gratifying to both of us, and often I would hang around until they took a break to continue to talk and encourage them. My personal journal entry:

"Wednesday, January 30, 2013, 6:15 a.m., Better Bagel Café. Assam, the shift manager was making his rounds, straightening chairs, wiping tables, sweeping crumbs and greeting the "regulars" by name. He paused near my table, caught my eye and smiled. I laid my ballpoint aside and said

"Sit down and tell me the Assam story!"

"What do you mean, 'the Assam story'?" he asked.

"Where were you born? How did you get here? Where are you going?

He smiled shyly, pulled back a chair and began to relate his birth in a foreign land, his arrival in the United States, a life-long financial struggle to get an education, purchase a car, and support himself, numerous setbacks and his goals. He had related all this without a pause or a prompt, then was suddenly self-conscious, that he was out of his role, intruding on my work and privacy.

"Assam, you seem to have a plan and persistence, both necessary to get ahead in life, keep up the good start."

"It has been wonderful to talk with you," he said. Then, haltingly went on, "It would be great to sit down and talk with you and other business people who come here if they would share their secrets of success." "O.K. When is your next day off?"

Then I received the letter from Windom High School.

chapter twenty-one
THE ADDRESS

Mom and Dad: I've have come back to Windom to speak at the high school commencement ceremony tomorrow. I plan to talk about our family and I will do my best to be true to myself, to honor you and to help the class of 2006 find their way in this complex world. And perhaps help us also.

Writing the letter had wrenched my innards. Now I felt emptied, spent but calm now pervaded my being. Feelings I had repressed for years were washed away in tears of relief.

I shivered. Was it the cool breeze or an eerie presence? I checked my watch, surprised that two hours had elapsed. Several tissues wet with tears lay at my feet. The sun was low in the western sky. I clicked on "save", sending my ramblings to a CD. It was growing late and I was growing hungry. I closed the laptop and drove into town to find some supper, then to make a few notes for tomorrow's talk.

The town looked the same and yet somehow different. Most of the local businesses are still located on the square, four streets all facing the court house. Gone was the "Corner Café", the bus stop for "Southwestern Stages" on its route from the Twin Cities to Sioux Falls. Gone was the Silver Dime Café where we played "Stardust" on the juke box for a nickel. The Chevrolet dealer had moved from the square to the outskirts of town, his spot now occupied by a furniture store. The First National Bank was now the town library and both Carlson's Grocery and Solemn's meat market had given way to supermarket chains down by the tracks. It appeared that my choices for an early dinner were fast food joints, Pizza, "Happy Chef", McDonalds and the teen hangout, "Hardee's".

Hardee's was near the motel and probably as good a choice as any. I could hear it from the parking lot and I entered to a blast of sound, music turned up loud, exuberant teens shouting over the music and the kitchen calling out orders on the sound system. If the food wouldn't upset me, the racket would. I ordered a salad and sandwich to go.

The motel was clean and featured standard motel furnishings…. queen bed, closet, desk, bath with shower and closet. I sat at the desk, replaced the 40 watt bulb with a 100 watt bulb, from my attaché case I pulled out my personal journal and wrote:

The past is past, and it is time to let go of it and live in the present, the here and now. You are not the little boy gratuitously spanked, lost in fifth grade fractions, humiliated for your interest in girls. I am not the boy from the cow barn to the classroom, a C- minus student. I am not the little brother, middle child nor pastor-preacher with co-opted sermons and playing a role scripted by others.

I am a man, a successful man who has blazed a new trail and been born again to share his gifts with the world.

I began to feel the strain and fatigue of the day. It had been a long trip on the road, an emotional experience in the cemetery followed by the sandwich washed down with a beer. I closed the notebook and opened the computer to begin tomorrow's talk, but my eyes blurred with fatigue. My mind was replaying the day's events and refused to focus on the task at hand. I removed my shoes, socks and shirt, pulled back the bed spread, flopped down for a nap and was soon asleep.

I awoke in the night with a start. At first I thought it was a dream. But it was no dream. There was a "presence" in the room and my father's voice: "I have always been proud of you Donnie, of your many achievements and honors, and I'm sorry I have not told you that. I thought you knew. I'm sorry for any thoughtless remarks that hurt you, that I did not stand up for you when you were teased and humiliated." Then he was gone. No one but Dad ever called me Donnie.

The theoretical physicist Michio Kaku was asked in a TV interview if he believed in an afterlife. He stated that the dead are still with us, that they exist in another dimension not normally available to us. Likewise, Elizabeth Lasser in her book "Broken Open" speaks of "visitations" where the dead return in some form to deliver messages to some of us. I believe.

I awoke again at dawn, sat at the desk and wrote:

> It can be a very disruptive thing for parents to
> have specific dreams for their kids.
> As I see it, a parent's job is to encourage kids
> to develop a joy for life
> and a great urge to follow
> their own dreams.
> The best we can do is to help them develop
> a personal set of tools for the task."
>
> Randy Pausch
> The Last Lecture

Parents with the best of intentions
make mistakes, hurt where they try to help.

Don Weir
A Parent.

YOUR FUTURE BEGINS TODAY
WHS Commencement Address
June 2006

Thank you, Superintendent Hill, for that kind and generous introduction. Thank you members of the school board, teachers, and staff for your twelve years of labor to bring about this celebration. Congratulations Windom High School class of 2006! I feel honored to be here today and to share this most important occasion in your lives, the lives of the graduating class, to the lives of your families, the life of this venerable school and the entire community.

As Superintendent Hill mentioned, I have some significant history with Windom High. My mother graduated in the class of 1920. My brother graduated in the class of 1943, I graduated in 1946, my sister in 1948, a niece in 1968 and a nephew in '72.

It was sixty years ago this week I sat in those very seats, a member of the Class of '46. I was not the valedictorian. I was not the salutatorian. I was "just let me out the doorian"! I do not remember the speech. I don't remember the speaker. What I do distinctly remember that as soon as that old guy shut up, Bob and I had a double-date to take a couple of cheerleaders to Arnold's Park. So if I see your eyes glazing over, I understand.

For the past 12 years you have been sitting in rows listening to older people talking at you, exhorting you, encouraging you, threatening you, and trying their best to equip you with the knowledge, habits, and methods to make the most of your lives. Now as your reward for enduring these threats and encouragements they have brought another old geezer to talk at you, to test your patience before you escape. So, fasten your seat belts.

In preparing for this day I decided that I cannot say all that I want in just one speech, so I am going to deliver two; one for your parents and one for you. Fear not, I will be brief. I remember Arnold's Park.

First, you parents, grandparents and other significant adults in your graduate's life, I ask you to consider an ancient text on this day of commencement. These are the words of Kahlil Gibran, the Lebanese prophet,. "Your children are not your children. They are the sons and daughters of Life's longing for itself. They come through you but not from you, and though they are with you yet they belong not to you. You may give them your love but not your thoughts, for they have their own thoughts. You may house their bodies but not their souls, for their souls dwell in the house of tomorrow which you cannot visit, not even in your dreams. You may strive to be like them, but seek not to make them like you. For life goes not backward nor tarries with yesterday."

I have chosen these words because history is filled with hundreds of examples of parents who attempted to impose detailed plans for their child's life followed by dramatic conflicts as the child seeks both to honor his father and mother, but also to fulfill his or her God-given mission, to discover and exercise her or his personal talents, to pursue the vision, the dreams of his or her own soul. We know many stories about George Washington, the father of our country, his brave soldiering, steering our government during those first, formative years. What many do not know that Washington's father died when the young George was 9 years old and his mother was so dominating that George tried to run away and join the British navy.

And in the world of fiction I know of no sadder, more tragic story than that of Neal Perry in the film, "The Dead Poets Society". Neal's authoritarian father planned his son's life in minute detail. He had enrolled him in Weldon Academy, an exclusive New England Prep School, that was to be followed by Harvard College and later, medical school. "You will be a doctor," he declared.

The film begins with Neal away at school and in defiance of his father's wishes, auditioned at the college theater where he won the role of Puck in Shakespeare's "A Midsummer Night's Dream." He loved the play. He loved playing Puck and loved the applause of the audience. Here, for the first time in his life he felt fulfilled, a sense of purpose and direction he had not before experienced. He felt appreciated for who he was. Neal announced to his friends that the stage would be his life. When Neal's father discovered that Neal had acted in disobedience to him, he summarily pulled Neal from the school and enrolled him in another school and threatened him to never disobey again. The film's tragic end comes with Neal so distressed and distraught that he took his father's pistol and ended his own life.

An example with a happier ending occurred right here in Minnesota. DeWitt Wallace was born in St Paul where his father was a professor of Greek at Macalester College. He urged young DeWitt to follow his steps on the path to higher education, but the boy heard an inner voice that led him to establish an enterprise you can still find on your news stand today. It is called, *Readers Digest*, with a circulation of thirty million copies per month.

I remember that Windom is a farming community and some of you here are farmers. I was privileged to be born on a farm to generations of farmers. We know that when we plant corn, we rightly expect the seed to produce corn. Plant beans and we get beans. Plant oats and no matter how hard we try to grow it into corn, it will remain oats, corn will grow corn and beans invariably come up beans. Likewise, when God sends you a musician, don't expect her to be a lawyer. When God sends you a scientist, don't expect him to be a preacher. And when God sends you a dentist don't try to make him professional ball player….not even a Viking quarterback! Look, listen and examine carefully the seed God has unto trusted into your care and keeping. It may take some time. Keep this treasured person safe, feed his or her body, mind and spirit and watch this one-of-a-kind person grow, mature, blossom, and ripen into the person God has placed in your care.

All of us who are parents and grandparents, take heart in the fact that parenting is not supposed to be easy. Listen to this wisdom:

"Parenting may be the most demanding task one ever undertakes, and for some of us it is with the least amount of instruction and the poorest models. Like flying an airplane without some instruction, the results may be tragic."

Now I speak directly to the Windom High School class of 2006. If I could only give you one sentence today it would be the advice Polonius advice gives to Laertes in Shakespeare's Hamlet, "This above all: to thine own self be true, and it must follow, as the night the day, thou canst not then be false to any man."

And to these words of the Bard, I would add Emerson's great treatise on Self Reliance: "Trust thyself! The great discoveries of science have come about because one man or woman has followed the convictions of his or her own heart and mind, stood against conventional wisdom and dared to be called an idiot or an infidel."

Both Copernicus and Galileo stuck by their inner convictions and their celestial observations that the earth turned on its axis and revolved around the sun. They were condemned by leaned professors and excommunicated by the Pope because all previous science and the church proclaimed that the sun revolved around the earth. Joseph Lister, the great English surgeon, was ridiculed by his colleagues for suggesting that infections from surgery could be reduced drastically by simply having the surgeons wash their hands. Columbus was laughed out of court when he proposed that the best way to the East Indies was to sail west.

He trusted his own wisdom, his own observations, his reasoning and judgment.

Another action that changed forever the way we live occurred on November 5, 1872 as hundreds of women tried to vote in the presidential election. The most famous of these was Susan B. Anthony who was arrested, convicted and fined for her effort. Refusing to pay the $100 fine, she stated, "Resistance to tyranny is obedience to God."

These are but a few of those men and women who, throughout history have dared to act on Shakespeare's admonition, "to thine own self be true" and responded to Emerson's clarion call, "And we are now men, and must accept in the highest mind the same transcendent destiny; and not minors and invalids in a protected corner, not cowards fleeing before a revolution, but guides, redeemers, and benefactors, obeying the Almighty effort, and advancing on Chaos and the Dark."

And I share with you my own long-held belief, that each one of us is sent here to this old world, this planet, with a mission, with specific work to do, and that each of us is divinely equipped with the necessary talents to accomplish that mission. For some of you it may be returning to the farm, producing food for an ever growing world population. For some it will be graduate school in medicine, music, engineering, law or teaching. Some here in this graduating class may not yet have a clear vision or understanding of mission….and that may well be because there is work to be done of which none of us here is yet aware. As I mentioned earlier, I graduated here in the class of 1946 and if any one of my class had declared that his mission was to be a computer programmer, or an astronaut, or a jet airplane pilot, we would have laughed him out of town or locked him up. But somebody had to be first, somebody had a vision, a dream and the will to try. So, if your goal is not clear today, if the end is not in sight, keep the eyes of your souls open, moving forward with your life, your education, your curiosity and keep your spirit open to the purposes of the Almighty. Yes, keep an open mind to the well-reasoned thoughts of others, weigh them against your inner truth, but do not waver, do not compromise for the sake of harmony or convenience. "This above all, to thine own self be true". Martin Buber said it well: "In the next life you will not be asked, 'why were you not more like Jesus' You will be asked, 'why were you not more like yourself.'" To this end I recommend that each of you make room for a time of silence, away from the noise of IPODS, twitter, Facebook, texting, TV, and learn to listen to your inner voice. Yes, there is an inner voice that is waiting to instruct and lead you into a life of intense satisfaction. It is the rare person who hears that voice early, who at age 8 or 9 has a passion to be a surgeon, or preacher, or farmer or musician or teacher or researcher. But to most of us, that comes later, often by struggle, sometimes against the counsel of others, often through trial and error. St. Paul wrote to the Christians in Rome, "Be not conformed to this world, but be transformed by the renewing of your mind." I like J. B. Phillips translation of that verse:" Don't let the world squeeze you into its own mold, but let God reform your life from within." When I was taught that verse it meant don't smoke, gamble, drink, play cards or dance, but that, I think, is just the opposite meaning of Paul's words, that is the world around you that includes parents, teachers, churches and preachers. Their advice and counsel is not to be ignored, but Paul says that the God who dwells within you wants to re-form your life, to birth that inner person that He has created and commissioned for service in this world.

To you graduates and parents alike, I invite you to consider the case of the teen-age Jesus. Never thought about Jesus as a teen-ager? Most of the Jesus stories begin with his birth, the Christmas story, and the next thing we read is his baptism by John and the beginning of his ministry. But Luke, Luke with the trained eye of a physician alone tells this story: Luke 2:41 ff. "Now every year his parents went to Jerusalem for the festival of the Passover. And when he was twelve years old they went up as usual for the festival." Luke does not explain that the trip to Jerusalem was several days walk, so for their safety and protection from robbers and other bad guys, Mary and Joseph traveled with a group of friends and relatives, the men leading the way in one group, (talking "guy stuff" no doubt), the women and children (including Jesus) following close behind, talking recipes and diaper rash and child care. At the end of a day's walk, they would separate into individual families dfor the night. Now listen to Luke: "When the festival was ended and they started to return, the boy Jesus stayed behind in Jerusalem, but his parents did not know it. Assuming that he was in the group of travelers, they went a day's journey. Then they started to look for him among their relatives and friends.

Now we understand why Luke tells us Jesus was twelve years old: he had made his bar mitzvah, the occasion when Jewish boys become men and assume responsibility for themselves. When they did not find him, his parents returned to Jerusalem to search for him. I like to imagine their conversation. Joseph: "If you had not been gossiping with those women, you would have watched the boy" Mary: "The lad has made his bar-mitzvah. You knew he should be with the men!" After **three days (Three days!! Can you parents imagine looking for a lost child for three days?)** they found him in the temple, sitting with the teachers, listening to them and asking them questions. "And all who heard him were amazed at his understanding and his answers." When his parents saw him they were astonished; and his mother shouted to him. 'Child, why have you treated us like this? Look, your father and I have been searching for you in great anxiety.' ' He said to them, 'Why were you searching for me? Did you not know that I must be in my Father's house?' Notice that Mary says 'your father and I have been worried" but Jesus replies,: "I must be in my Father's house. Luke notes that Jesus lifts the title of Father from Joseph and rests it with God" But, Luke reports, " they did not understand what he said to them." Now there is a line familiar to most of us: they didn't understand him. Then, Luke reports, he went down with them and came to Nazareth, and was obedient to them. His mother treasured all these things in her heart."

It would be convenient for all of us, parent and child, if that transition happened in a moment or a day or in a commencement service. But it usually occurs over stressful time with a series of thrusts towards independence and followed by retreats into dependence, and on a given day we never know whether we are speaking to the child or the adult.

One of the most…if not the most… important decisions you will be making over the next years is the choice of a life mate. (Some of you may have already made that choice). This is not only an important pursuit of your life, it is perhaps the one that is most fraught with peril, loaded with opportunities to make a total mess of your life. Our country is a graveyard of failed marriages and the resulting trauma to mates, to children and to career and financial success. This year would be a good time to think through…and put in writing…the characteristics you want in a life partner, as a parent for your children, who share your hopes and dreams for a fulfilling life. I too often see infatuation with dimples, orthodontia, biceps and other body shapes and freckles be mistaken for love. Infatuation is great…I wish for everyone that springtime high, But when the body parts of the parent of your children begin to droop, when wrinkles form on the face and gray hair begins to thin, character needs to take over where cute no longer rules.

O.K. only one more minute:

Whenever I have to make a speech or write an article or a book, I stop to realize that smarter people than I have already thought about this subject, spoken about it, written about it. So I close today with these words from a guy you all know. His name is Steve Jobs, founder and C.E.O. of Apple Computer. He says,

"Your time is limited so don't waste it living someone else's life. Don't be trapped by dogma…which is living with the results of other people's thinking. Don't let the noise of others' opinions drown out your own inner voice. And, most important, have the courage to follow your heart, your intuitions. They somehow already know what you truly want to become. Everything else is secondary."

If you thought your exams are over, I leave you with one final question: "Sixty years from today when you are standing at this lectern, what will you say to your grandchildren?"

Windom High, class of 2006, congratulations. God bless you.

chapter twenty-two
POST SCRIPT

"Honor your father and your mother
so that your days may be long..."
Exodus 20:12

Parents and graduates alike seemed attentive to the talk, responding with generous and enthusiastic applause. The superintendent and school board members who hosted the Distinguished Alumnus Award luncheon were lavish in their expressions of gratitude.

When I had shaken the last hand and acknowledged the final accolade, I slid under the wheel, snapped the seatbelt and took a quick tour of the old home town, once around the courthouse square, then I turned south on Fourth Avenue, once a link in U.S.71, then crossed Highway 62 into Island Park where the ancient dam still held the Des Moines river at bay, creating a broad river that formed the western boundary of the city. The park featured a well-maintained picnic/playground area, a log cabin built by an early settler and now restored to its nearly original condition, and finally the high school football/soccer field. The cadence of the marching band and the roar of the crowd at a Friday night football game echoed in my mind.

Enough! I eased the Cad out the gate and turned right up the hill to the cemetery again, parking where I had parked yesterday. I opened the laptop and continued to write.

I came here yesterday ready to forgive you for the wrongs I perceived that you had imposed on my life. Now as I recount the hardships and sacrifices you both made to provide for our family during the '30s, the many sacrifices you made to give me an education, and which I took for granted, I here offer my belated and deepest thanks. I ask your forgiveness for the perceived wrongs I have harbored rather than showing gratitude for the support and help you gave me. In my preoccupation with a search for self, with the inner struggle to be born again I failed to take into account your 8th grade education, Dad, and that you did the best you knew how. Dr. Benjamin Spock was not yet in medical school when I was born. You were doing what you knew, what your parents did and what the community standards were.

163

So I ask your forgiveness for the negative thoughts I have harbored over the years, for my failure to take the lead in opening deeper conversations and dealing with the unexpressed feelings and longings of your hearts and mine. I realize now that you did the very best you knew how.

I am ashamed for my selfishness, my lack of appreciation for the many sacrifices you made that I could go to college and seminary. You bought clothing and bedding for college, new luggage, a typewriter and most of all, tuition, board and room. And let me not fail to mention that you gave up a hardworking, dependable and knowledgeable farm hand. Forgive me for expecting you to do more than you knew how. I, too, did only what I knew how. I did not know how to, or felt intimidated to communicate my feelings, to bypass the taboos of the time and place.

You both taught me life lessons I am now only beginning to appreciate; the importance of perseverance, the respect for the earth and all its creatures; the value of one's character, the fidelity of one's word, the compassion towards those less fortunate. The high esteem in which you were both held in this community as people of faith, totally honest, true to your word, caring for your parents in their final days are traits to be emulated..

I hope my speech today did not offend or embarrass you in any way. It was meant to honor you. It was meant to help the graduates and their families avoid some of my blunders and to help families to listen deeply to one another, to share and support each other's opinions. It caused me to remember that I always had your undying support even when you did not understand the directions of my life. Thank you for all that you *have done to support me even when you did not understand me.*

"I thank my God every time
I remember you ....."

Philippians 1:3

Your loving son, Don

I saved the letter to CD, popped the disk out of the laptop and carried it to their headstones. With blinding tears blessing their remains, I pressed the disk deeply into the sod between them. A sense of closure settled over me as I knelt between them and I lingered briefly feeling cradled in their love. Healed!

I returned to the car, loaded the CD player with a Handel organ concerto and headed south. From somewhere deep in memory, Robert Frost spoke:

I have promises to keep
and miles to go
before I sleep.

The End

ABOUT THE AUTHOR

Windom High School 1946, Univeersity of Dubuque, BA 1950, Dubuque Theological Seminary, M. Div. 1953, Chaplain U. S. Navy 1953-1975, Real Estate Broker 1975-1998. Published articles Presbyterian Life, Young Miss, The Real Estate Professional, Tra-Navy Personal Journaling.

The book, "Heretic Son" is a memoir providing plenty of this ... a lifelong struggle to free myself from the fundamentalist,beliefs of parents and find a new Christianity.

Married Beverley Hoy, Newport, RI 1959, 2 children Diane Ridley, and David, two granddaughters and one great grandson. Live in Maitland, Florida. Volunteer for Adult Literacy and Meals on Wheels.